EVERYDAY MIRACLES

EVERYDAY MIRACLES

*Meditations on Living
an Extraordinary Life*

ARDATH RODALE

RODALE

© 2007 by Ardath Rodale

Rodale books may be purchased for business or promotional use or for special sales. For information, please write to:

Special Markets Department, Rodale, Inc.,
733 Third Avenue, New York, NY 10017

Printed in the United States of America

Rodale Inc. makes every effort to use acid-free ♾, recycled paper ♻.

Book design by Tara Long

Library of Congress Cataloging-in-Publication Data

Rodale, Ardath H.
Everyday miracles : meditations on living an extraordinary life / Ardath Rodale.
   p.   cm.
   ISBN-13 978-1-59486-601-2   hardcover
   ISBN-10 1-59486-601-5   hardcover
   1. Miracles.   2. Spirituality.   I. Title.
   BL487.R63   2007
   646.7—dc22   2007011495

Distributed to the trade by Holtzbrinck Publishers

2 4 6 8 10 9 7 5 3 1 hardcover

RODALE
LIVE YOUR WHOLE LIFE™

We inspire and enable people to improve their lives and the world around them

For more of our products visit **rodalestore.com** or call 800-848-4735

I DEDICATE THIS MESSAGE

STRAIGHT FROM MY HEART TO ALL

WHO ARE STRIVING TO BRING

HEALTH, HEALING, LOVE,

AND UNDERSTANDING TO OUR

TROUBLED WORLD.

CONTENTS

LIVING—AND LOVING—EVERY DAY

Part 2

CELEBRATING YOUTH

Part 3

GIVING THANKS

Part 4

ENCOURAGING HOPE

Part 5

Caring for Yourself and Others

Part 6

Feeling the Seasons

Acknowledgments

To my family and all my eleven grandchildren, who are the delight of my life.

To Lois Hazel and Chris Potash, my editors; Liz Perl, my publisher; Mark Kintzel, who is my right hand and great friend. Mike Krajsa, who is my sounding board for many new ideas.

Ms. Hiroko Koyama and the Shumei organization, who gave me a whole new horizon, and Chisako, Tokiko, and Yasushi, who always lift my spirits.

The beloved camp children who visit my farm every summer and who keep me young at heart; my Mennonite neighbors, who remind me to keep life simple; and special *Prevention* readers like Jocelyn Cook from New Zealand and Marji Marazi from New Jersey.

The ten smiling Japanese children who visited with me, and The Rodale Institute's wonderful South Korean interns.

Seattle Smith, a new friend, and John Toya from Jemez Pueblo, who named me "White Feather."

There are so many more people who help make a difference in my life, the employees of Rodale Inc. and The Rodale Institute—they are all valued and loved!

About the Author

Ardath Harter Rodale, Chief Inspiration Officer of Rodale Inc., beautifully articulates the company philosophy: "Our mission is to show people how they can use the power of their bodies and minds to improve their lives. 'You can do it,' we say on every page of our magazines and books." She also serves as cochairman of the Board of the Rodale Institute—a global leader in organic agriculture, food, and health whose mission is to promote their program for Healthy Soil, Healthy Food, Healthy People® worldwide.

In 1985, Mrs. Rodale's son, David, died from AIDS, prompting her to become an AIDS activist. Currently, she is a member of the Harvard AIDS Institute's International Advisory Committee.

Mrs. Rodale holds a Bachelor of Science degree in Art Education from Kutztown University. Her numerous honorary degrees include two Honorary Doctor of Humane Letters degrees, one from DeSales University in Allentown,

Pennsylvania, and the other from Lehigh University in Bethlehem, Pennsylvania; an Honorary Doctor of Laws degree from Kutztown University in Pennsylvania; and an Honorary Doctorate of Humanities degree from the New College of California in San Francisco.

She has been honored by local, state, and national organizations, including the Outstanding Alumni Award, Kutztown University; Valley Forge Freedoms Foundation Award for Humanitarianism; Extraordinary Voices Award, Mothers' Voices (National), New York; Women of Distinction Award, Great Valley Girl Scout Council; Friend of Lehigh Award, Lehigh University; Lifetime Community Achievement Award, Boys & Girls Club of Allentown; Shining Star Award, St. Luke's Hospital, Allentown, Pennsylvania; Life and Breath Award, American Lung Association; Exceptional Woman Award, Women in Periodical Publishing, New York; LifePath's Community Service Award, Pennsylvania; The "Circle of Excellence—Enlightened Media" award from the International Furnishings and Design Association; Lehigh Valley's Coalition for Alternative Transportation (CAT) award for promoting alternative transportation, especially bicycling, to youth and adults.

Mrs. Rodale was named as one of the 50 Best Women in Business in Pennsylvania by the *Central Penn Business Journal* in 1996 and as a Distinguished Daughter of Pennsylvania by Governor Tom Ridge in 1997. She was chosen as one of the top 50 Women Business Owners in the United States in the October 1997 issue of *Working Woman* magazine and as one of the 50 Leading Women Entrepreneurs in the World by The Star Group in 1999.

Ardath, usually known as Ardie, is author of three books, *Climbing Toward the Light*, *Gifts of the Spirit*, and *Reflections: Finding Love, Hope, and Joy in Everyday Life*, published in 1989, 1997, and 2002, respectively; she also writes "Reflections," a monthly column for *Prevention* magazine. Ardie was one of twenty-nine prominent women whose thoughts on the role of spirituality in modern life were featured in the book *Embracing Our Essence: Spiritual Conversations with Prominent Women*, published in 1995 by Health Communications, Inc.

She is the mother of five children and grandmother of eleven.

Introduction

I have a Celtic harp in my living room. Two of my grand-children were fascinated and wanted to play, but it was badly out of tune. They were eager to find out how it could be tuned so they could play. In a joint effort one child pressed the designated piano key, and the other child pressed the foot pedal as I tightened each string on the harp. Each time I asked them to tell me when they heard the two tones sounding as one. "Yes, yes, we hear it! It's a miracle." This was not only a lesson in tuning an instru-ment but also a lesson in life. In order to play beautiful music in our lives, we need to think of ourselves as finely tuned instruments.

Now translate this to what happens when all the instru-ments in an orchestra play in harmony. A community of players creates a masterpiece to bring joy and appreciation to others. It is exciting to know that music is therapy for people with many kinds of illnesses. Music can touch the sensitivity of our souls to heal our emotions and spirit.

Some of us will never master playing an instrument, but we can appreciate hearing a master musician play. In my teen years, I played the violin, not well, but I enjoyed playing in the school orchestra. When I hear a maestro playing magnificently, I become that person in my mind. My fingers move nimbly over the strings as the bow glides, tenderly creating music to warm my heart. It surrounds me with love and peace.

Many other creative expressions have similar potential—visual arts, voice, dance, and drama. Some of the most beautiful and miraculous music comes from nature through the song of birds and the rustle of leaves in the wind. Even the sound of a distant train whistle, the crunch of snow beneath our feet, or the laughter of children adds to our natural symphony. Every day we can all be receivers of these wonderful gifts.

Look at the potential for each one of us to create, to interpret, to appreciate, to share, to influence positive change in the world. Let your mind be inspired, your body stretched with energy, and your spirit touched with love.

You are not ordinary, you are extraordinary. Listen to and play the music of your life, and your miracles will begin!

Everyday Miracles

Part 1

LIVING AND LOVING
EVERY DAY

SAVORING
MOMENTS OF JOY

*M*any days lately seem to be too filled with "stuff."
I asked a young man yesterday how his day went, and he
said, "It started bad and ended bad. It's all work." Sometimes I feel like this, and I'm sure you might, too.

Another young man at our company recently said, "I
can't believe that people a few doors away from me send
e-mail messages instead of coming to talk to me face-to-
face." Seeing a smiling face can be a moment of joy!

I remember the words from a poem by William Words-
worth:

The world is too much with us: late and soon,
Getting and spending, we lay waste our powers:

4

Little we see in Nature that is ours;
We have given our hearts away, a sordid boon!

....

For this, for everything, we are out of tune

Yesterday I felt like this, too. I had to break the pattern. There is a house in the woods where I sometimes go. The warm sun was streaming in the window. I pulled up a chair to shed my cares instantly and savor moments of joyful peace. It was as if the world stood still. There was not a sound to be heard. I tried to get in tune with myself and the world.

There are such little things that in our rush we might overlook that can bring joy. Picking one flower—even if it is a dandelion—can change the tide of our exhausting thoughts. Look around to see what natural joys you can discover.

The way you start your day can direct your thoughts to those of joy. How about giving your partner, child, or pet a good-morning hug instead of rushing out to the day's activity? This act of love can bring a feeling of warmth for both of you that can stay with you all day long. It's a moment of joy knowing that you are cherished. Tell "You" that you are loved and are a special treasure—a child of God.

Living alone, I have found a way to bring joy at the end of the day. I put on soft music and pick up Puss Cat in my arms. We sit on the rocking chair together, and I hum to the music. She relaxes in my arms. I feel her warmth and purring love, and it brings pure joy!

Above all, as you go through the day, remember to smile. The spark in your eyes is a message to everyone you meet that you know the joy of living.

At the end of the day, count up the moments of joy you experienced and appreciate all the good things that have happened. Be thankful for your gift of life and your opportunity to reach out to make a difference. Your gentle touch is a gift of joy!

EVERY TIME
A BELL RINGS

*S*ome time ago, I had to be in the hospital for a day. While I was there, a bell rang and a cradle song was played throughout the hospital six times—even in the elevators. I finally asked a nurse why this happened. She told me that it was a happy announcement that a baby had just been born!

Sometimes bells ring loudly and clearly, while at other times they ring softly and delicately. Do you stop to listen to the innuendos, or do the sounds of bells become an accepted background for living?

As I sat in my sunroom on a beautiful, frosty winter morning enjoying the peace, my solar chimes began to ring, reminding me that the sun was shining. I felt happy and thought about the importance of bells through the ages and their meaning to us now as they bring joy and inspiration to our lives.

Before the common person could read or write, people relied on village bells to convey important messages. They were signals to those working in the fields that it was time to eat or end their day's work. Vendors used bells to announce their arrival in towns to sell their wares, and bells also called children to school. In some rural areas, bells are still attached to animals' necks by herders so that those who stray can be found.

Bells remind us of time and of those things that are timeless, universal, and eternal.

Clocks chime the hours of the day. Alarm clocks jar us from a good night's sleep, telling us to wake up and greet the day, hopefully with optimism. Doorbells can be exciting sounds as we greet family and friends. Dinner bells remind us that it's time to gather for refreshment and to count our many blessings.

Bells call us to worship and toll when someone dies. Wind chimes remind us to pay attention to the air around us that is the breath of life. The Liberty Bell is a reminder to cherish our precious freedom. Singing bowls from Tibet can be a call to meditate and attune ourselves to the great vibrations of the universe. Bell choirs bring joy to the spirit through the eternal medium of music.

Perhaps the most important message of the bell is that it is asking us if we know what time it is—are we in the morning, noon, or evening of our lives? By being in tune with our surroundings, we can be truly alive and excited and look forward to making the most of each new day.

In the movie *It's a Wonderful Life*, when a tiny bell on the Christmas tree rings, the little girl tells her father, "Teacher says that every time a bell rings, an angel gets his wings."

Listen to the pulsating bell in your heart that awakens the angel in each of us. Spread your wings, and let your spirit ring!

THE BUTTERFLY OF LOVE

One year I was so worried because I hadn't seen any butterflies, and I was concerned that environmental conditions might be causing them to disappear. I felt sad.

Several weeks later, my good friend, Mark, called me, very excited. He felt that he had truly seen a miracle at a magical place—a property our family owns—that is located on top of the mountain near our offices. Wildlife is plentiful there, with lots of deer, wild turkey, and birds of all kinds. A house sits silently in the clearing in the midst of this nature conservancy. It is a place filled with unbelievable peace and beauty.

Behind the house is a rock garden planted with butterfly bushes. To his amazement, Mark saw the bushes covered with butterflies. He counted five different varieties. He said, "Oh, Ardie, if only I had brought a camera!"

The next day, I took my camera to see this beautiful sight. The butterflies glistened in the sunlight as they busily flitted from one flower to the next. I felt such awe at our precious world and lingered for a long time.

This reminded me of another very special event. On a bright, sunny day, eleven years ago, my daughter, Maria, was married in the moon garden on the farm where I live. The service was so touching. At the end of the ceremony, some of Maria's sisters distributed envelopes to people sitting in the aisles and, when Father Gambet gave the word, the guests were told to open the envelopes. As a smiling Maria and Lou walked down the aisle, monarch butterflies flew up and away out of the envelopes! People cried tears of joy!

At the end of last summer, we had a family dinner outside on the patio of a restaurant. It had rained, and my eight-year-old granddaughter wandered down to the pool. She found a rain-soaked butterfly that couldn't fly. She gingerly picked it up, put it in her hand, and brought it back to show us. Like a mother taking care of a loved child, she tried to nurture it back to health. As we left the restaurant, she carefully showed it to many of our friends who were dining there. They were fascinated. The next day I went to a party attended by quite a few of those same friends. Very excitedly, the first thing they asked was, "How's the butterfly?"

I answered, "It's still alive!"

And so is this beautiful world of ours—alive and growing more precious each moment. Let the butterfly remind us to appreciate all our blessings in life and to hold close with love, and care for, the fragile world around us.

New Horizons

*W*ow! You've come this far on life's journey. How does it feel? Congratulations as you face the next path before you. Rodale promotes the message, "You can do it!" You are on your way to new horizons. Are you ready?

I love Walt Whitman's poem, "Song of the Open Road":

Afoot and light-hearted I take to the open road,
Healthy, free, the world before me,

The long brown path before me, leading
wherever I choose.

Take with you on your journey the excitement for what you might discover each day.

Be amazed at life—and enjoy each other. It's the magic that keeps us young at heart.

Stop to observe the richness around you—our beautiful world, your family, those you love.

Keep hope alive as you anticipate success and see yourself already there.

Create your own style. You are your own special artist as you create your own masterpiece.

Be honest and tactfully kind.

Congratulate someone when they are doing a good job.

Volunteer and share your talents with others.

Reach out with love and be a gracious receiver.

Stretch way beyond what you are capable of so that you can grow and understand more tenderly what life means. These challenges are like solving a puzzle as all the pieces fall into place.

Touch with tenderness.

Change life from inside you and pray that by reaching out with love, you can help others heal their hearts and the world.

Keep fit by balancing the mind, body, and spirit. Remember that your body is your cathedral where you honor your most important treasure—yourself. All that you are is a garden that needs nurturing to produce beauty and abundance and value. Know that you are a majestic human being.

Life is a gift, a celebration, an opportunity we have been given. A long time ago, I heard a speech by a thirty-year-old woman with AIDS. She concluded her speech with: "The best we have is right here in this moment. The love we hold in our hearts is here and now."

Look up! The sun is shining on your path. Now is the time for *you* to take that open road! 🌿

MIRACLES

*H*ave you ever thought about the miracles in your life? They might come upon you like a bolt of lightning or land softly on your shoulder. They are unexpected joys, surprising coincidences, amazing beauties that you want to hold in your heart to treasure forever. I have been writing them down to use as inspiration when I feel sad.

In the past year, I have found miracles beyond measure. It's *you*, my readers and cheerleaders! Many of you have found gleanings of ideas and inspiration from what I have shared with you from my heart. I am honored that many of you have taken these thoughts and energy to a higher plane and have shared the results with your friends and with me.

After reading my essay "The Elegant Spirit," Linda from Arizona left me a voice message to tell me that before she went to sleep, she wrote down twelve beautiful, special thoughts she wanted to remember.

Jocelyn from New Zealand left a voice message saying that she had shared "The Elegant Spirit" with her family at a get-together. They all wrote down what was beautiful in their lives, and then all twelve people shared what they had written. This was followed by a very touching letter accompanied by gorgeous inspirational photographs she took illustrating some of her favorite passages in my books *Gifts of the Spirit* and *Reflections*.

There is a whole chorus of readers from all over the United States and Canada who sing together in fond memories "Jesus Wants Me for a Sunbeam." When I mentioned this song in "Sitting in a Sunbeam" (February 2003 *Prevention*), I received not only the words but also the music from many readers.

Lisa from Oregon sent me a very touching children's story she wrote called "Grandma's Rainbows."

Anne from Missouri sent me little magnetic strobe lights that can be clipped on or worn in the hair or as a necklace. They are a delight to children and adults as a reminder to let their lights shine!

Majda, a native of Slovenia now living in Colorado, has

shared the most delicate little note cards she makes of dried flowers. Each one is a miraculous work of art.

Lou from Montana sent me a poem by Patricia Lynn Reilly titled "Imagine a Woman," from her book *Imagine a Woman in Love with Herself* (Conari, 1999). It has a very special meaning for all of us as we strive to make a positive difference in the world, in our communities, and within our families. I put the title on my refrigerator so I don't forget this important message.

I have a very special bronze statue of a child sitting on a rotating pedestal that signifies the world. She is covered with a blanket of leaves. Her cupped hands reach out to be a receiver, but also a giver, of pure love.

What we do in our lives can have a tremendous ripple effect as we reach out to touch others. How lucky we are to have each other. Can you feel my hand reaching out to touch you with gratitude and love? 🌹

LOVE AND HEALING

I am always lifted up when I attend the Japanese Shumei Celebration in Pasadena, California. There is a positive spirit of joy and the ability to rise above problems. I feel renewal in my soul. Shumei spreads love and light.

At a special session, I was asked to speak with a group of women who are either current cancer patients or survivors. We shared what we have learned, lifted each other's spirits, and decided to have a network of encouragement for one another. What was apparent was that we can rise above feeling bogged down by illness and adversity. Our minds can be affected by our pain. It is important that we find ways to learn through it and overcome it.

In *Shumei* magazine I read about a man who was being treated at a hospice whose director, Dr. Harada, gave this wonderful advice: "This material world is just like a school—that is to say, an 'earth school.' We have a lot of chances to learn from everything that happens to us. Even sickness is a valuable message from God. Why not become friends with it? Even if you have an illness, you can live meaningfully, better than before. It is important for you to accept your sickness in your heart."

Chisako, a Shumei member and good friend of mine, told me about a mother and daughter who lived in an apartment across the hall from her. One day she saw the child limping and asked the mother what was wrong. The child had developed a brain tumor, and Chisako asked if she could perform Jyorei—a healing art in which spiritual Light is focused on others—for the child each day before and after school. Three weeks later, the child had an appointment with her doctors, who were amazed to find that the tumor was completely gone!

When I receive Jyorei, sometimes tears fill my eyes as I feel the stress leaving my body, and my heart is filled with the feeling of being one with the universe. I count my blessings of love of family, friends, and pets, and extend the soft touch of love to all.

Fling open the door to your heart and then with a joyful smile reach out to make a difference, bringing peace, love, and healing into all that surrounds you in life!

Part 2

CELEBRATING YOUTH

Our Children

*A*ren't children exciting to be with? My heart melts when I see them so full of life, curiosity, and happiness. They are our most precious gift.

Perhaps sometimes in our rush, we forget that they are the future of the world and how we nurture them will determine what kind of citizens they will eventually become. We want children to learn how to get along with each other, appreciate diversity, and hold our earth and each other sacred.

Yet, I wonder if we aren't shortchanging young people when I read articles in the newspaper about the alarming rise in obesity in children over the last twelve years. Recent news reports quoted the Surgeon General as saying that the nation's obesity epidemic has gotten so bad it soon may overtake tobacco as the leading cause of preventable deaths.

USA Today ran an article about the importance of encouraging children to drink water instead of juice or soft drinks. These are just a smattering of the articles that have come out recently concerning the health of our young people.

I am concerned about what I see at the supermarket—carts loaded with snack and convenience foods that will be just popped in a microwave. Not only children but adults have lost contact with food and where it comes from. Ancient Ayurvedic philosophy teaches the importance of touching food and forming a spiritual bond with it. My son, Anthony, once said, "As long as you have the smells of home, you'll always come back."

The Shinji Shumeikai, an organization in Japan, has developed a huge program to teach children about food. They tell them, "Touch the earth, touch the food gently."

The Rodale Institute has developed a fantastic traveling exhibit titled *Healthy Soil, Healthy Food, Healthy People*® designed by my daughter-in-law Florence Rodale. It is interactive and teaches children the cycle of good nutrition from start to finish. It opened at the Capital Children's

Museum in Washington, DC, and has been traveling to many parts of our country. Adults, too, find the exhibit fascinating.

The Rodale Institute also recently launched the Kids Re-generation Resource Network™, an exciting, Internet-based electronic magazine aimed at children ages 7 to 13. It provides tools that will inspire young people around the world to regenerate not only the soil but also their own physical, emotional, and spiritual wellness. Tuning in to the section on Natural Movement, you'll find terrific exercise ideas for kids to do outside. There are craft ideas, especially for paper sculpture, that demonstrate how children can make critters or plants to build their own indoor garden at home. I invite you to visit kidsregen.org.

I found a wonderful little anonymous article, "What Shall We Give the Children," which asks what we can give children as they travel life's road: ". . . no toy or bauble will do. It must be something more. . . . It must be devised out of responsibility and profound caring—a homemade present of selfless love. Everything changes but the landscape of the heart."

Hold the children gently and teach them how to be healthy and that their bodies are sacred. Help them discover the beautiful and lovable pearl within their hearts. ✿

FIREFLIES

Summer is the time for delightful magic. I'd like to share with you one of my favorite times. As the evening deepens, the fireflies come out to light the world. Through the years, I often pretended that they were fairies carrying lanterns to their tiny dwelling places—too small for our eyes to comprehend.

Several years ago, my granddaughter, Shelbi, was showing her two-and-a-half-year-old cousin Eve how to catch fireflies. Eve was fascinated by this phenomenon. Several days later at dusk, she went outside and, in her tiny voice, cried, "Fireflies, where are you?"

A friend told me the story of his three-and-a-half-year-old daughter, who said to him, "Look! The fireflies are feathers in the sky!"

I found this quote from Rachel Carson: "If a child is to keep alive his inborn sense of wonder without such gift from the fairies, he needs the companionship of at least one adult who can share it, rediscovering with him the joy, excitement, and mystery of the world we live in."

I wonder how many of us are that kind of companion to our children, grandchildren, or the children in our neighborhoods. Do you marvel at your sense of inner creative joy that looks at everything as though you were seeing it for the first time? I guess most of us rely on children to help us adults see things in a new light; we use them to refresh our sense of wonder. Let's also find joy in helping them fuel their creativity. What an exciting adventure to embark on together, hand in hand.

Over the years, I have received so many letters from *Prevention* readers sharing their thoughts and prayers for my health. They are like the glow from fireflies lighting the path toward wholeness for me. I am so grateful that they took time to help me explore new perspectives on the healing process. They renewed in my mind the need to bring back more creative time in my own life.

Know that creativity in whatever form—writing, painting, cooking, building, storytelling, gardening, etc.—takes us to a higher plane, lifting our spirits and strengthening our healing energy. Just think of the inner glow that we can radiate outward to help mend the world!

As the evening draws its curtain of darkness, please take someone by the hand and go out to gaze in awe at the stars above and the fireflies below. It's the perfect time to imagine, to weave stories, and to speak softly, heart to heart. Remember that our own light is a beacon illuminating our soul with magic and spreading joy and hope in the night! 🌱

FEEL THE LIGHT

On one particular Saturday morning, I wanted to feel light in my life. I asked myself, "Where in the house is the best light to read the morning paper?" Usually I do this at the kitchen table, but I need an overhead light. Then I saw the perfect place. Because the dogwood tree outside my living room window was still bare, the room was bathed in glorious morning light. As I sat in my favorite chair, there was a rainbow on the back reflecting from the crystal on the credenza under the window.

With delight, I sat down there and said to myself, "I'm sitting in a rainbow of light!" I felt warm and peaceful. There was not a sound to be heard. Instead of reading the paper, I just sat enjoying this blissful feeling and allowing my mind to wander.

My chair is surrounded by children's toys that are silent now. Perhaps I should put them away. There are a hutch and a cradle made for my grandmother by her father many years ago. There are handmade toys from my childhood and a wonderful wooden rocking horse made for my children by my husband Bob. There are building blocks that children used to build castles and towers with their imagination, marble roll-downs, a small Irish harp, and other great toys belonging to my children and grandchildren. I feel the light and wealth of joyous times, each one holding memories, remembering laughter and the touch of busy hands. I feel the light of love. I know in my heart that there will be other children who will come to this corner with happy, smiling faces. I look forward to those times.

I thought about the correlation of the toys surrounding me and the waiting with anticipation of spring awakening our earth once more. Sometimes it's hard to wait to see the earth come alive. We believe we can really smell the damp spring earth; and, as we close our eyes, we imagine all the beautiful flowers that will bring cheer to the now barren soil.

But we have today! We have the opportunity to share

that feeling of delicious light by reaching out to touch children, our families, friends, and those who are ill or grieving, the hungry, the homeless. We can stretch out our hearts and hands to share our warmth and appreciation and care so that they, too, can feel the light of love. 🐎

PRECIOUS

Olivia Golden, formerly with the Children's Defense Fund, was quoted as saying, "We've been neglecting our youth for so long we are now in a crisis for all ages. But research has shown that young people with problems can be rescued." We can help our society heal.

This is a call to parents, grandparents, teachers, and young people to wake up! Through the years, as a teacher, mother, and grandparent, I have watched children growing up, and I suspect that many problems with young people today are caused by our fragmented society. We view problems as if we were looking through a microscope, homing in on the nucleus while the surrounding areas are hidden from view. For instance, government, some schools, and parents have begun attacking the difficult issue of obesity, but this is only the tip of the iceberg.

My son, Anthony, often said, "As long as you have the smells of home, you'll always come back!" There is a wonderful nostalgia of coming to your door, anticipating a great meal because of the delicious aroma.

Is this the kind of seduction our young people have today for a home-cooked meal? Too often because parents are hurried, there is a take-out meal brought home or a frozen meal that is popped into a microwave. No wonder children pop food into their mouths without joy. They eat the main course without the appetizer of anticipation.

Self-esteem holds the key to lifestyle changes—what it comes down to is whether or not someone truly values himself or herself. I speak to young people in many schools, and I have compiled a list of ways that they can help themselves—actually this can be a list for you and me, too!

- Treat yourself with special care as you would treat a best friend.
- It's okay to be who you are. You need only to be in competition with yourself to make a better you.

- Throw away resentments you might have for others.
- Say "No" to risky behavior.
- Eat well and take your vitamins. Your body is a sacred temple.
- Realize how much your family loves you, and say "I love you" often.
- Concentrate on what's right about yourself instead of what's wrong; this is the true mark of a healthy person.
- Keep optimistic.
- Make a commitment that you want to live—everyone has dreams and talents that we all need to make a better world.
- Care about each other.
- Be thankful for all your many blessings.

Health is achieved when we establish a balance of mind, body, and spirit. This is what we need to teach our children and then give them the tools to make it happen. We need to light the lamp of hope and excitement in young people—many of whom have little hope or love and appreciation for how special they are. Children are the richness of the world. Each one should bear the label "PRECIOUS," and that's the label for you, too!

EDUCATION—
THE HUMAN TOUCH

The arts—visual, performing, musical, literary—are often the first thing to be cut from school and government budgets. Just at a time when children's minds are most open and creative, we close them down by removing artistic, creative endeavors from their daily schedules. Yet these are the subjects that open young people's minds to nurture a healthy spirit. Beethoven said, "Music can change the world."

Our educational system often stresses math and science over music and art, but we need to emphasize both right- and left-brain activities if we want our children to grow into well-balanced adults. Science and art need each other. Studies have shown, for instance, that children who study a musical instrument before age ten actually do better in math and science than those who don't study music.

Creative ideas affect the emotions of the heart and allow us to dream and hope for a better quality of life. They help us look at life with beauty and inspiration, with purpose and vision. For me, every night I watch the beautiful sky and look for new horizons. Connecting with nature and this marvelous world fills me with ecstatic awe.

A family I know had five boys. Throughout their youth, their mother would have them sit at the kitchen table, each with ample paper and a large tin of crayons to promote drawing as a way to stimulate their creativity. At the same time she encouraged them to sing. It was a joyful time for them all and helped each of those boys develop in their own unique way into adulthood. We need to encourage this kind of activity in our families and our schools.

Today's children spend a good deal of time on computers, computer games, and TV. The computer is a great learning tool, but wait!

Educational psychologist Jane Healy presents a different view. In her book, *Failure to Connect: How Computers*

Affect Our Children's Minds—For Better and Worse (1998), Healy stresses the importance of waiting until children reach the age of seven before introducing them to computers. After taking a look at the potentially harmful effects of computers on child development, she cautions that "the minute we introduce an artificially engaging stimulus with fast-paced visuals, startling noises, silly scenarios, and easy excitement, the brain is diverted away from its natural developmental tasks."

Creative activities open neural pathways and increase our ability to "think outside the box" and solve problems resourcefully. Our children will need this ability to be leaders in the future. Sometimes dreams start small like a beam of light in the midst of the fog.

James Truslow Adams says, "A poet or a painter or a musician does not say to himself, 'I will make a million first, and then I will write poetry or paint pictures or compose music.' His art is life itself, the best of life."

HANDS—A MOST
PRECIOUS GIFT

*P*lease look at your hands. They are a history book of where you've been and everything you've touched and worked for. Think of the handshakes you've shared and pause for a moment to remember how they felt—some weak or strong, others soft or rough. Through their hands, you felt some of the other person's character and even the kind of work they've done. Remember how your hands feel when you hold a small baby or someone of any age. They are filled with love and beauty.

I remember the hand of a kind hospital intern comforting me during a spinal tap procedure and, another time, the hands of a nurse who had tended my dying son cradling my face as she calmed and consoled me before a serious operation.

You are probably familiar with the famous painting *The Praying Hands* by German artist Albrecht Dürer. There is a meaningful story about it. Being an artist was Dürer's fondest dream. He had another artist friend, an older man, and the two of them struggled together to stay alive. The friend told Dürer to continue painting, and he would go out to work. When funds came in from selling the paintings, he said, he would begin painting again himself. Sadly, the friend who labored to support them developed enlarged joints and twisted fingers that made it impossible for him to hold a paintbrush. One day, Dürer saw his friend kneeling in prayer. He said, "I can never give back the skill in those hands, but I can show the world the feeling of love and gratitude which is in my heart for his noble deed." Now, those praying hands have inspired people all over the world.

At the summer children's camp on our farm this year, one little girl had an accident, and other girls gently stroked her hair, trying to comfort her. I carefully laid my hands on her injured leg and told them that hands can help heal. "Can they really?" they asked, and I said, "It happened to me." A calmness spread over the injured child.

The camp children are so spontaneous and loving. When they see me coming down to the farm, they cry, "Ardie!" and run with outstretched hands into my waiting arms for hugs. Look at what our hands can do!

Please hold your palms upward to receive special gifts of love and kindness. Now turn your palms downward and feel that you are giving back love and kindness through service to others.

May our lives be a blessing as we reach out spreading joy and sharing peace, hope, healing, and love in *every* season of the year. I reach out to touch you!

INDIGO CHILDREN

All through my growing-up years, my father said in exasperation, "Ardie, why don't you be normal?" I didn't feel loved. I wanted to be loved for myself. Parents often don't deliberately inflict pain on their children but react to the pain in their own lives. Did you have the same message from one of your parents or teachers?

I am concerned about some school structures today that try to make all students fit into the same mold. Often it is the academically gifted person who gets the most attention, but not everyone learns the same way. In our society today we need to encourage diversity, creativity, and imagination as well.

We need to have parents and schools teach social skills—the gentle touch, kindness, and the importance of exploring new landscapes for each of us. We need to connect with our glorious outdoors and touch, feel, and imagine a beautiful world of peace.

In 1982, Nancy Ann Tappe, a San Diego parapsychologist, wrote a book called *Understanding Your Life thru Color.* She noticed the emergence of children with a deep blue aura—Indigo Children—and reasoned that the vibrant color signaled the dawn of a new consciousness.

James Twyman produced a film, *Indigo,* about how to raise Indigos, and it shows mostly happy, intelligent children who are academically gifted and talented in the arts. An article titled "Indigo Theory Sees Children in a New Light" recently appeared in our local newspaper, showing characteristics of Indigo Children that may include:

- Psychic skills and awareness of the paranormal
- Having Attention Deficit Disorder or autism
- Functioning best when alone or outside with pets
- Feeling a special purpose in life
- Having difficulty with absolute authority

➤ Expressing strong angst about pollution or government corruption

The most popular book about Indigos, *The Indigo Children: The New Kids Have Arrived* by Lee Carroll and Jan Tober, says that telltale traits of an Indigo include a feeling of "royalty" and that they "deserved to be here." Indigos "see better ways of doing things."

I realize now that I was an Indigo Child.

Imagine a beautiful world of peace! *Imagine* the news media filled with exciting stories of people inspired by new ideas of life and love. Let's bring a fresh, invigorating vision of change for our children and the world! ➤

Part 3

GIVING THANKS

THANKS FOR LIFE!

*A*woke up this morning with my mind calling me to sing, "Let it shine, let it shine!" I heard these words to a song many years ago, and it left a lasting impression. Opening up your mind to shine means to me to make room so that the depth of your mind can be filled with appreciation and ideas for well-being. It is a wonderful gift to be able to wake up in this light! "Good morning, Life! I greet you with love. It can be Thanksgiving every day!"

Native Americans feel that all life is sacred. Every day nature can fill us with new discoveries of the beautiful and precious. Notice not only the grass but also all the different kinds of plant life that make up the grass. Observe the process of planting a seed from its birth to celebrating its glory in bloom and its glorious harvest of the fruits of the field to nourish our bodies and souls.

The miraculous changing seasons give us inspiration to help alter our regular routines by granting us fresh vision as there are challenges to be faced. We are thankful that we have the opportunity and the ability to turn difficult times into harmonious endings.

Let us never forget that we are caretakers of our world as we work together to regenerate the land and the environment so that it is a safe place for our children, grandchildren, and generations to come. We are thankful for our amazing world.

We are thankful for family and friends who remind us that we are not alone. We are here to help each other, to rejoice together, to be sad together, to be an arm to lift each other up to face life again.

We are thankful for the love that draws us together as we work for causes to bring the world closer in unconditional love and for the ability to grow toward a clearer light of understanding for what it means to be human.

May we be touched not with dying embers but with the torch of flaming love. Reach out with action to live from the heart as, by our touch, we care for one another.

Thanksgiving is a two-way street. We are grateful for

the privilege of being able to give to others, and we appreciate what comes our way. One day while recuperating from cancer, I sat with a huge stack of letters and well wishes. It was an absolute amazement to me that so many people cared. As I sat there, I said out loud, "This is like the breath of life. As I breathe in, I am filled with all these positive thoughts, and, as I exhale, out goes all negative thought."

Thank God for each new day that is given to us as a precious gift to treasure!

A WALK IN THE SUN

A morning walk is my best tonic for beginning each day. As I walk early each morning over the farm, I step into the sun. I'm sure I hear you saying, "But sometimes the sky is filled with heavy clouds." To me, the sunshine is in my mind and heart. I feel that each day is a special gift to be filled with joy, appreciation, and love.

I'm always eager to discover something new. To hear the chatter of birds makes me want to join their chorus. Their cheerfulness fills me with energy as I watch their busy activities of gathering food or building nests. I'm like an excited child when I see bulbs peeking through the soil.

Some days it's an unexpected surprise to see an intricate spiderweb that wasn't there the day before stretched across my path. The finely woven threads glisten in the sun.

Other days, as my lungs expand with the exercise, the scent of the moist earth dampened by dew or rain the previous night arouses fond memories of walking in the woods, camping, or wandering by a cool, rippling stream. I remember college days with nostalgia when spring came, and I could hardly wait to go out with my umbrella and roam the full length of the long Main Street.

The local park near my home is a great place to enjoy nature. I watch squirrels scurrying for food, and I laugh at some of the spunky dogs trotting on leashes at their masters' sides. Most important, though, are the many people who greet me with a smile and friendly "hello." Even when I don't know these fellow travelers, I feel a closeness as we reach out to let our spirits mingle.

When I return from any walk, I'm filled with gratitude for the privilege of being alive in this beautiful world. I feel ready to face the day in the larger community as I carry with me and impart to others some of the energy and peace I find on that walk. Our challenge each day is to share the healing touch of all this natural glory of living. All we have to do is open our hearts and let the sun shine in!

CELEBRATING THE TEMPORARY

Celebrate the Temporary by Clyde Reid stresses the point that too often we are preparing for tomorrow or living in the past while we miss the wonderful experiences and joys of today.

Have you walked barefoot in the grass in the early morning dew? My granddaughter, Maya, and I did just that one day on my farm. The cool, soft grass felt so wonderful beneath my feet as I visualized my carefree days growing up. We laughed, we ran, we were quiet. We walked through the garden, smelled the flowers, and dashed through the sprinkler—a relief from the day's heat. We stuck our feet in the stream and let the soft silt squish through our toes.

That same day, I went to a special retreat in the mountains. I continued to play the inquisitive child and experience the moment. I wondered if I could stand submerging my bare feet in the spring-fed pond in front of the house. Screaming with delight, I felt a shock of exhilaration and instantly recalled the rhododendron-circled mountain pond of my childhood—the only place we had to swim—an isolated spot we shared only with the trout.

The next evening, Maya and I continued our excitement at my farm. She pleaded to visit the Mennonite neighbor to see the cattle. My eyes darted back and forth between one of the Mennonite girls and Maya. Maya and I felt the strong golden braid on Ida's head and then felt the fine silky hair on Maya's head. Mother Laura's hair was barely visible under her Mennonite cap, but smiling with pride she said to us, "You know, my hair is like Ida's and, when I let it down, it touches my waist." It was my turn to admire.

We headed back, stopping to see one blue egg in a robin's nest and, finally, enjoyed a bath to wash away the grime but not the memories.

I will never forget these experiences, spending the happiest moments seeing life through the eyes of a child.

Maya's inquisitiveness was spontaneous and enriching. Who says we have to live in an adult world? Only we as adults put limits on our experiences without realizing that we still have most of the world to discover. The challenge is there. It's a wonderful way to relax by taking time and celebrating the temporary today!

GRATITUDE AND GRACE

like to think that gratitude and grace are like my two hands working together. Grace is the power, beauty, and love of God that is always around us, but gratitude gives us the eyes to see it.

Native Americans teach their children to wake up being thankful for each new day. Their philosophy has greatly expanded my well of gratitude. I try to find something new and precious to appreciate in nature every day. Even the cycle of planting a seed, watching its progress to full bloom, and then its decline to sleep beneath the earth fills me with thanks for the privilege of being part of nature's miracles.

Elaine Hubbard wrote that gratitude is one of the great

positive emotions because it creates magnetism. A magnet draws things to itself, and, therefore, giving heartfelt thanks for all the good around us makes us attract *more* good into our daily lives.

Helen Keller said, "I thank God for my handicaps for through them I found myself, my work, and my God."

Life's journey is never totally smooth. We all will encounter mountains and valleys along the way, but in the hard climb up the mountain or the difficult descent into the valley, we learn life's lessons and become stronger in character. Be grateful for the challenges you face because they help you grow, help you understand, soften your heart, and give you strength.

I have found in my life that it is vital to start my day with thankfulness. I begin with exercises and affirmations every morning as I get out of bed. I look out my bedroom window to see a bronze statue of a beautiful woman lifting a child to the sky in her outstretched arms. It is here that I express my gratitude for family and friends, praying for their health and happiness. As I name each person individually, I raise my arms like the statue and enfold my loved ones in healing, kindness, purpose, safety, energy, peace, and love. Then I extend my arms to include all those in the world who are ill, grieving, stricken with AIDS, orphans, the homeless, hungry, and sad, and our sacred environment.

When we say "thank you," we open our eyes to all the miracles around us.

Ramakrishna says, "The breeze of grace is always blowing on you. You have to open the sails and your boat will move forward."

And Henry Ward Beecher said, "God's grace is the oil that fills the lamp of love."

Grace surrounds us like the soft, comforting, refreshing rain. Let gratitude help you find the power of that grace and see all your experiences in life as blessings.

May you journey in peace!

Let's Walk Together

A tree, a road, a hillside,
And a white cloud drifting by—
Ten men passed along that road,
And all but one passed by.
He saw the road, the tree, the cloud
With an artist's mind and eye,
And put them down on canvas
For the other nine to buy.

Anonymous

*D*riving to work, I see people of all ages walking with a fast, determined pace while wearing headphones. I wonder if they are only listening to what someone else is saying, or do they enlarge their healthful thinking as they strengthen their physical bodies?

J. I. Rodale and his son Bob, my husband, often walked the fields alone, allowing their creative minds to fill with ideas for improving health for themselves and the world.

Walking is really like taking a journey through life. It can lead you up and down many roads. While we tread most paths alone, there is joy and a sense of purpose when we share that path with someone else. My heart melts when I see an older couple walking together holding hands with love, or when I see a trusting child holding the hand of a parent.

When we walk together, we have the opportunity to share our talents, laughter, and loving hearts with each other. As we walk arm-in-arm with someone, we can support each other, sharing happy or sad times and lifting each other up.

Life is a spiritual as well as a physical journey, and we can nourish the spirit in each other, allowing it to grow on its own path as we make progress in understanding and adapt to what we learn on our path together.

In the Lotus Sutra, the Buddha taught that cause and effect are simultaneous; that is, for every thought, word, or deed you make in life, the effect is already waiting for you. Your actions today create your future. When you participate in a walk for a charitable cause, for instance, you *become* a force to help others while you improve your own health at the same time.

Whether you journey in rain, snow, or the warm brilliance of the sun, *how* you walk the path determines the meaning of your life in this world. Do you walk hand-in-hand, heart-to-heart, arm-in-arm, spirit-to-spirit, or do you rush along, head down, seeing only the ground before you?

Let's slow down, lift our heads, stretch out our arms, and embrace fellow travelers, thankful for their companionship and for the opportunity we have to reach out to touch them.

Shed the weight off your shoulders, breathe deeply, and smile. It's so good to be alive! 🌹

Joy!

Hello, Joy! I need you today! I guess I have gotten in a rut with too much to do and my nose too close to the grindstone. Sometimes my days are too directed by the "have to" list.

Jeremy Rifkin said in his book *Time Wars* that the modern age has been characterized by the restless energy that feeds on speed, records, and shortcuts. Despite our alleged efficiency, we seem to have less time for ourselves and far less time for each other. We have become more organized but less joyful.

When I feel at a low point, I finally remember that I have cut out the time for creativity and renewing my soul. How about you? Do you ever feel this way?

No one can do this for us. It needs to be like a cool, gushing spring that spouts out from inside of us, bringing a rush of well-being. I liken it to the old-fashioned water pump outside the door of my great-grandmother's house in the country. The icy pump water replaced dry heat with refreshing coolness. Perhaps we could call this bringing ecstasy or joy into our lives! Abraham Maslow discovered that people felt fulfilled in their lives when they were motivated not by need but by the desire to grow.

Margot Anand wrote in an article in *Body + Soul* magazine that, as the daily assault of modern life wears us down, more and more of us long for healing and for new ways to connect with our spirits and feel joy in our lives.

Each day the sun rises on new adventures and sets on wonderful memories. It brings new life with every sunrise. I feel like I want to run with the wind, let my bare feet touch the green grass covered with dew, stretch my arms open wide, and then bring them close to feel that sun and hug those people and animals I love.

I am truly grateful for my family and for all my friends—old, new, and those I've made through writing for *Prevention*—who are there to touch my life and fill me with joy.

As I write this, there is an old camp song that keeps racing through my mind. It begins something like this:

I feel the joy, joy, joy, joy down in my heart
Down in my heart, down in my heart to stay.

Our feet are earthbound, but our hearts and our minds have wings.

Bandleader Les Brown said, "Shoot for the moon. Even if you miss, you'll land among the stars!"

Part 4

ENCOURAGING HOPE

LOOKING FORWARD

Winter is a time when most of us look inward at our lives. Perhaps we evaluate where we have been. Then spring comes, and at this time of year, I never cease to have renewed excitement as I anticipate the sprouting of bulbs and flowers as the sun heats up the earth. Perhaps you feel like I do—so full of hope.

The dictionary defines hope as "to expect with desire; a belief in fulfillment." Enthusiasm is all we need to make each day a fantastic and positive experience. How about starting the day with a smile and thoughts that rays of sunshine will fill your face and mind with happiness? Then, watch the effect on each person you meet. It is true that a hopeful attitude helps us see and experience the best in life.

Hope can also help you cope in times of trial. A teacher was sent to a hospital to help a badly burned boy with his grammar lessons. At the end of the session, she felt she hadn't done a very good job, but the next day the hospital staff asked what she had done to change the boy's response to healing. Two weeks later the boy told them that when the teacher came to help him, he thought, "They wouldn't have sent a teacher to help me with my schoolwork if people thought I was dying."

In the magazine *Hope*, the editor began one of her editorials, titled "Hope in Action," by writing, "Each of us has the capacity to create the world we want by starting with the most ordinary of human acts."

Fill your life with hope, love, and action. Believe, pray, and never lose faith that you can change the world. *You* can do it! You can bring hope and healing to our troubled world: touch with kindness, one step at a time.

Here are some tips to awaken hope in your heart:

➤ Visualize your dreams for the future.
➤ Relax and see your burdens dropping away.

- Stretch mentally to challenge yourself for the good that is yours.
- Breathe in all the beauty that surrounds you.
- Breathe out and look for one good quality in each person you meet.
- Walk with your head up, looking for the joy in life.
- Talk with kindness to one less fortunate than you.
- Love others to exercise your heart.
- Pray to communicate with your God for peaceful direction.

An old proverb states, "It is hope alone that makes us willing to live."

When Aristotle was asked what hope is, he answered, "The dream of a waking man."

CHALLENGES AND CHOICES

*W*ouldn't it be great to waken each day to feel really alive and filled with positive energy and hope? This is what we all dream for our lives, and it can be for your life. It's a matter of challenges, introspection, choice, and growth. We can chart our course.

In my own life, I have faced tremendous challenges. The biggest happened when my son, David, died from AIDS. I worked hard as an AIDS activist to remember his life as a celebration of unconditional love and one that could help people of all ages to understand and be educated about that dread disease.

Four years later, I was diagnosed with breast cancer

and had radiation treatments. Five years later, my husband was killed in Russia in an automobile accident, and I took over his position at Rodale. Three years after that, my cancer came back. This time I had a mastectomy and no other treatment.

Within three years, I had been diagnosed with another form of breast cancer. This time I have opted for no chemotherapy. For the past twelve years, I have read all I could find about cancer and alternative treatments. There is extensive information from sources around the world, including early publications of *Prevention*, and much of it now is beginning to be accepted by the medical profession!

My oncologist has been treating me with letrozole (Femara), a hormonal therapy. My integrative medical doctor prescribed a host of herbs including mistletoe injections, a combination of Japanese mushrooms, and DIM, which is a concentrated form of cruciferous vegetables, immune boosters, and other vitamins. I have kept both doctors well informed, and they both accept each other's treatments.

I've often questioned why this happened to me when I am careful about leading a healthy lifestyle and eating a healthy diet. I always come back to the role of stress and the fact that I have a hard time pacing my tremendous energy.

I heard a famous doctor, Bernie Siegel, tell a true story about one of his patients who was diagnosed with inoperable cancer. The man refused chemotherapy. Seventeen years later, he returned to the doctor's office.

"You are supposed to be dead," the shocked physician told him. The man replied that when he received his diagnosis, it was spring, and he knew it was time to plant his beautiful garden.

The love of gardening has always played a big part in relieving stress for me. I visualize my mind and body as a beautiful inner garden, too, and feel hopeful.

The most amazing experience happens continually now. Even people I don't know very well will stop to tell me that they wish me well. I am so deeply touched by these people reaching out because in many instances they need care more than I do. Sometimes we share a warm hand or a hug. Tears roll down my cheeks as I feel the love and care we have for each other.

Let's reach out every day to share our inner garden, where we can help to plant understanding, faith, hope, and love in each others' hearts.

THE STRENGTH WITHIN

etween the brick wall of my patio and the macadam of the driveway, I saw a tiny green shoot appear. Each day, I watched it grow. How was the seed planted there, and where did its nourishment come from? It grew tall and finally blossomed into a cleome flower that lived until the frost. Plants, while appearing to be frail, must have the strongest will to live. That is the power of hope. Normally we think of strength as a quality of lions or athletes, but we can find it in the least likely places. It is within you!

I remember a story from my college days of a poor, sad-faced little Russian boy dressed in rags who was secretly playing on a $1.75 violin his mother had bought him at great sacrifice. His father was against his son "fiddling away his time." Encouraged by his mother, he persevered, using every spare minute to practice. That little boy was the famous Rubinoff, a violinist whose $1.75 violin was replaced with a real Stradivarius in later years. He was like the cleome growing outside my door.

Do you remember seeing producer Francis Ford Coppola's movie, *The Secret Garden*? Mary, a lonely child, grew up in India and was orphaned at ten. She was sent to live with her uncle in an austere castle in England. At night she was sure she heard a child cry, and upon investigating the sound, she discovered a cousin her own age; Colin was confined to his room as an invalid. Everyone around him told him he was sick and was going to die. Mary said defiantly, "If everyone told me that, I wouldn't do it!" She encouraged him to live by telling him of a secret, overgrown garden on the estate that she and another young friend were trying to bring back to life. They took Colin there in his wheelchair and taught him to walk and play. The garden became a healing balm for Colin and his father, who had given up hope for his son.

Dore Schary, playwright and motion picture executive, quoted her mother as saying, "If you have a weakness, make it work for you as a strength, and, if you have a strength, don't abuse it into weakness." Have you ever made a list of your strengths and weaknesses? What insight would you gain if you applied Schary's quotation to your list?

When you face obstacles, remember that you have the resources to find strength within yourself to overcome them. Strength is in each of us and is nurtured by faith, perseverance, and thankfulness that leads you toward a purpose and a desire to move forward. Just like the tiny green shoots, you can push your way through any obstacle and climb toward the light.

As Hans Christian Andersen's Thumbelina says, "Nothing is impossible if you follow your heart."

ABOUT FACE

*D*o you remember the wonderful story of *Gulliver's Travels?* Jonathan Swift wrote this amazing story in 1726. It was a political and social satire exposing the ways that man sinned against the clear sight of nature and goodness.

I picked up a video to reacquaint myself with one part of the story and discovered that the message is still very pertinent to life today. It was a story about love, fear of the unknown, power struggles, and the senselessness of war between two countries.

Gulliver was shipwrecked on an island and dragged himself with all his strength onto the beach, where, exhausted, he fell asleep. Tiny people—the Lilliputians—inhabited the island, and their fearful town crier discovered Gulliver and hysterically alarmed everyone in the town that a giant on the beach was a spy. They tied Gulliver up while he slept.

Meanwhile, King Little and King Bombo were busy signing the marriage contract for their two children, Princess Glory and Prince David, who were deeply in love. Each king insisted on his own wedding song. Finally David's father, Bombo the warrior, declared war, and the two lovers were brokenhearted. Havoc took place.

Gulliver won the hearts of the Lilliputians with his kindness, but King Bombo's spies were ordered to kill Gulliver with his own gun. David intervened by jumping on the gun, and both David and the gun fell to the bottom of a ravine.

Gulliver picked up David and said to the sad, distraught kings, Look what you have done, King Little, by being thoughtless and selfish. King Bombo, you were too busy being the mighty warrior. What did you gain? We can settle this peacefully by turning malice into a melody and combining the two wedding songs:

"Faithful forever . . . we may be apart now and then, but I'll hold you in my heart 'til you're in my arms again."

Have we changed throughout the ages? It is time in our lives that we grow beyond the barbaric concept of war and find alternative ways to deal with conflict—not only with other nations but within our own hearts.

May we look at our lives with peace and an understanding of our differences as we find ways to appreciate each person's uniqueness through sharing, caring, loving, and forgiving. Look up! The sun is shining in your heart. You can make a difference to help heal our ailing world and each other!

> *"Many are the ways to share*
> *The mystery that is me,*
> *And the greatest of these is Love."*

—Danaan Parry, *The Essene Book of Days*, 1996

MIRROR, MIRROR ON THE WALL

One of our readers wrote to me recently mentioning the importance of mirrors, and her letter made me think. A long time ago, my aunt said to me, "When I look in the mirror, I don't like what I see." I can remember my youngest brother standing in front of a mirror making faces at himself. When I asked what he was doing, he replied, "I'm telling myself a story."

We tend to take our mirrors for granted as we busily get ready for work in the morning or prepare for bed at night. We often glance at our reflection, but do we really see ourselves?

Did you ever think of your mirror as having a soul,

reflecting back to you your feelings? Has your mirror ever said "Good morning" to you, or, better yet, have you said "Good morning" to your mirror? When you look in the mirror in the morning, do you see the weight of unresolved problems carried in your mind through the night? Or do you see your smiling face as you anticipate joy in the coming day?

Your smile, your frown, your eyes, your dreams, your heart's desire are all reflected in your mirror. Stop for a minute and say hello to your soul friend who is looking back at you. Smile, and you will always get a smile in return. Ask yourself, "What is my dream for today? What can I do to make my dream come true? I will get rid of all doubts because I want my dreams to live."

Recently I attended an Omega Institute "Being Fearless" conference in New York. One speaker mentioned that we are our own mirrors expressing love. Another said that we are like seeds planted in the garden of our minds, and we can grow messages to keep heaven inside us.

Every morning, when you look in the mirror, you plant a seed for that day and for the future. The growth of those seeds will show you how well you live and love. Just by loving yourself, the whole world opens up. Each of us has the choice to be what we see in the mirror!

Remember to put your best face forward when you look in the mirror. Throw your shoulders back and breathe deeply. Be confident and tell yourself, "I can rid myself of fears and worries!" Hold your head high and face your feelings, knowing that you can be seen, understood, and *loved*!

Every day you can have sunshine in your heart. Tell your mirror image the words of Maya Angelou, "I am working toward a time when everything gives me joy!"

Welcome your friend—the *mirror*!

THE CONSTANT GIFT

PART I

We have all seen the devastation wrought in our world these past few years. People have reached out in so many wonderful ways to help others who are suffering. The big tragedies make the evening news, but we often do not hear about the quiet tragedies that are part of everyday life for so many people living in impoverished countries—people and families who have lost hope and often die from malnutrition.

Several years ago, I was intrigued by the ingenuity of an organization called Heifer International (Heifer) that is reaching out to change conditions in such places. Its mission is to end hunger and poverty and to care for the earth by giving families a source of food rather than short-term relief. Heifer gives self-reliance and hope to millions by providing each family an animal and training them to care for it. The result is that the animal—which may not be killed—becomes an ongoing gift to others as families pass on the offspring, by-products, and training of their animals to others in their communities.

"Animals join the project family circle. . . . The family knows that the survival of the animal is directly related to their own improved quality of life," says Dr. Terry Wollen, director of animal well-being.

President and CEO Jo Luck says, "Heifer teaches our project participants: take care of your animals, and they will take care of you."

One year for Christmas, I decided to give an "Ark." For my donation, I received cards for one dozen animals and asked each of my grandchildren to choose an animal they would like to give. They put a lot of thought into their choices and felt a deep sense of pride in knowing they had personally helped a family in desperate need.

In 2005, Mike Krajsa, a professor at DeSales University in Center Valley, Pennsylvania, took a group of students to Cuchuma, Peru, to work with Heifer. One of the students, Brian Radziwill, wrote, "I see my experiences with

Heifer International as the most valuable in my life. Different cultures, values, and beliefs should not scare even the most timid of individuals. It is only when our faith and values are tested that they become stronger. Only together can we solve many problems that exist in our society."

There are many organizations, like Heifer, that provide people with the means to support themselves and also to care for our precious environment. Won't you consider a donation to such a worthy cause?

Learn more about Heifer on their Web site, www. heifer.org, or call them toll-free at 800-422-0474.

THE CONSTANT GIFT

PART II

*P*lease sit down in a quiet corner and contemplate how you can be a spreader of sunshine this year.

Spread your love and care as if you are sowing seeds of kindness and watch them grow. You can change any ordinary day into a day of miracles by your positive outlook. It begins with the sun in *your* heart. Look outside. Wrap your arms around yourself and say out loud, "I love you. Today will be a beautiful day!" Realize in your heart that you are worth it. Fill your lungs with fresh air.

Greet your family members in the morning with a hug and an "I love you!"

Tell those people you work with that you appreciate

them and hope they have a good day. Listen with compassion if they have a problem.

Send appreciative, encouraging notes to people who are doing a good job.

Call someone you haven't spoken to in a long time and wish them well.

Visit someone who is lonely or ill or send them flowers.

There are other simple things you can do like cutting grass, running errands, grocery shopping, baby- or pet-sitting, cooking, or lending a hand with paperwork for someone coping with overwhelming personal tragedy.

Recently I attended the funeral of a man who was ill a long time. His father came to the service. It was the first time he had seen his son in many years. Can you imagine the heartache that could have been healed through forgiveness?

There is a wonderful book (later made into a movie) by Catherine Ryan Hyde called *Pay It Forward*. The main character, twelve-year-old Trevor, decided to change the world by doing an extraordinary favor for three people in his life. When they ask how they can repay him, he tells them they must "pay it forward" by doing a big favor for three other people. Although this book is fiction, it became a popular idea and now there is a Pay It Forward

Foundation (www.payitforwardfoundation.org) that encourages people, especially students, to put this concept to work in their lives.

Imagine a world like this where people are committed to helping one another every day without expecting something in return!

When you give these special gifts of hope, support, love, and strength to others, you encourage them to do the same. Then, the sun that shines in your heart will spread out to all.

Here's a letter I sent to the children who attended Rodale's summer camp, encouraging them to "pay it forward" by being scouts or leaders in their own special way.

CHRISTMAS 2005

Dear Camp Friends,
Happy Holiday Season!

Do you remember the letter you wrote to yourself? As promised, I am sending it back to you. I've been thinking a lot about each one of you and remember your smiling faces. In my mind I still hear, "Hi, Ardie!" as you greeted me here on the farm. Now it is so-o-o quiet!

I have a very special gift for you. It is a Sacagawea gold dollar coin. The English translation of her name is "Bird Woman." She was a Lemhi Shoshone Indian who, at the age of fourteen years, with her baby strapped on her back, was the scout who led the Lewis and Clark expedition through the northern Great Plains to the Pacific Ocean between 1804 and 1806. Her bravery and spirit can be an inspiration for each one of us.

Did you ever think of yourself as a scout, that you could be a big help to someone else? Perhaps a person in your family or a friend needs help.

Please keep this coin in a safe place to help you to remember the message of being a scout—or perhaps you can call it being a leader.

You are a very special person who can do great things.

You are part of the sun when you smile and bring happiness to others.

You are part of the stars as you give your family and friends new ideas—for this, too, is being a scout.

Love,
Ardie

Part 5

CARING FOR YOURSELF
AND OTHERS

Your Heart's Garden

*A*re you fascinated, as I am, by all the documentation that is being published about the experiences of some heart transplant recipients? What amazes me is that some of these people take on certain characteristics of their heart donors. What happens to some of these people who have a new lease on life suggests that the heart has a memory, and that memory can be transferred.

Recently, I went to Canyon Ranch Spa in Lenox, Massachusetts. I had been really stressed and knew I needed to heal. Joan Berry, the counselor, led me through three sessions of "Healing Touch." It became apparent that I had some blocks in my mind and heart that needed to be released if I wanted to be healthy.

I began to visualize that my heart was a very sacred inner garden. As I placed my hands over my heart, I could feel warm energy being released. I saw the correlation between my heart and planting and tending my garden outside my home. As I take care of my outside garden, it is with tender loving care that I place the seeds and the plants in the warm soil. Through the season, I nurture those plants to blossom and flourish so that they can produce fruit and beauty to nourish my body, mind, and spirit.

Then I realized that I could give the same tender care to my sacred heart's garden! I contemplated how I could strive to make it the most beautiful place in my body, and I share my thoughts with you.

- Plant positive action and pull out the weeds of negative thoughts and anger.
- Plant forgiveness and gentleness.
- Encourage diversity. The most beautiful gardens have a variety of color and plants of different heights and growing habits. We need to nourish each one's intention to grow in its own way.
- Fill the heart with kindness so that the blood, as it travels through your body, nourishes every single part.

✣ Most of all, just love your heart tenderly. As you
breathe deeply, feel it expand with openness and joy
as you release blocked-up emotions you don't need
anymore.

Who knows? Someday, you may donate your heart to
someone who needs a new lease on life. You will be giving
the best heart that you can give. In the meantime, you have
given your own body the priceless gift of a heart light that
shines with brilliant, healing energy! ✿

Loving Your Mind

*H*ave you read *The Little Prince* by Antoine de Saint-Exupéry? One of the lessons of this charming tale is that it's only when you love something and care for it that it becomes unique. You become responsible for the thing you love.

Do you ever stop to think what a priceless treasure your mind is? I guess most of us take it for granted. We are caretakers not only of our own minds but also of our children's.

I was shocked to read in the newspaper a while ago that studies suggested that television might overstimulate and permanently rewire the developing brains in infants, and cause an increased risk of having attention problems by age seven. The problems cited in the article include difficulty concentrating, acting restless and impulsive, and being easily confused.

Looking back to my childhood, I had a tremendous variety of experiences to investigate and help me grow. Those experiences were valuable not just for seeing new and interesting things but as opportunities to expand my mind and connect to other facets of life.

Another article on research conducted by Sonia Lupien, PhD, a gerontologist at McGill University in Montreal, concluded that people who have low self-esteem actually have smaller brains than those people with high self-esteem. Dr. Lupien's advice is to build your self-esteem in order to increase your memory performance.

We can have healthy bodies, but if our minds are not healthy, it is a tremendous loss and affects the whole body's performance.

Olympic champions spend quiet time before competitions concentrating, focusing, and visualizing their complete performances. Coaches feel that this is even more important than the last-minute physical practice of their routines.

What can we do to love our minds? We can fill our minds with positive challenges—I know that writing this essay was a challenge for me (!)—appreciation, joy, and love. Each of us needs to realize how special it is to have a precious mind. The outcome is like a rare jewel that can be polished to its full brilliance. Imagine that you are that rare jewel, and reach out to develop your full potential.

Loving life is loving your mind!

OVERBOOKED AND OVERWORKED

A recent article in Canada's national newspaper, *The Globe and Mail*, was titled "Multitasking—The Next Great Curse: Self-Inflicted ADD at Work." It says we're increasingly hyper-distracted with e-mail, the Internet, and work. Experts tell us it's important to get unplugged before we become unglued.

Dr. Edward Hallowell, author of *Crazy Busy: Overstretched, Overbooked, and About to Snap! Strategies for Coping in a World Gone ADD*, says the more tasks we try to do simultaneously, the less effective we become in doing them well. Symptoms of attention deficit, he says, could describe just about everyone in the workforce.

While we're told multitasking is a valuable skill, the brain isn't wired to handle a rush of competing chores.

Dr. Hallowell suggests writing a list of activities and rating them as either highly creative or marginal uses of time to help identify unnecessary tasks.

Ms. Beth Herrild, a Seattle-based career consultant with Quest for Balance, says that chaotic times are often predictable. When you anticipate a heavy schedule, postpone taking on new assignments and take time to appreciate yourself. Today people don't slow down enough to feel they've done a good job.

Here are my suggestions for bringing calm when your world is too hectic.

- ➤ Picture your problems as a small weightless feather in the palm of your hand and blow them to the wind. Watch as they are wafted away to land on new territory.
- ➤ To relieve your mind before bedtime, jot down what you need to remember so that you can rest peacefully.
- ➤ When you're stressed at work, get a change of scenery. Go outside and let nature touch your heart and mind. Touch the earth. Hug a tree. Take deep

breaths. Say to yourself, "Thank you. I am alive and well."

➤ Meditate for twenty minutes each day.

➤ Listen to soft music, embrace yourself, and remember you are special and can contribute to a healthier world.

➤ Reach out to loved ones. I think back to when my children were small and full of unbounded energy. Though they were tired, they wouldn't stop. As I held them lovingly, rocking and humming to them, their frenzy gradually changed to peace.

We can do this for children, family, and friends now. Touch one another tenderly, feeling the warm quilt of relaxation and love surround you. Perhaps this is the most powerful stress reducer of all. ✿

OPEN YOUR WINDOW

*H*ow often do you come home at the end of the day exhausted? Do you ever stop to think how you might be shortchanging your life? Perhaps you might have trouble sleeping at night. Many of us have forgotten the daily rhythm of the body—breathing in and breathing out. Think of the lesson of the ocean waves: the tide comes in like our daily schedule and, as it goes out, there is a period of rest. This is a calmness that we need in the ocean of ourselves. Recall what nature has to teach us. Open up the window of your soul to exhale and let the calm envelop you.

Why should you do this for yourself? There are lots of articles appearing in magazines, books, and programs in the media that stress that bottled-up feelings can cause illnesses of all kinds. Take time to think about it. How can you bring more meaning to your life?

There is an increase in the number of people who are taking time to attend retreats. In 2005 alone there were 2.5 million people who made the effort to look for more meaning in their lives, so go on a retreat if you can or take "mini-respite" time. This is a pause that gives you an opportunity to question more deeply, "Where am I going in life?" It's a period to be comfortable being alone and to get in touch with your feelings that might have become buried in the rush through life's complexities—a breathing space where you can nourish your soul to grow.

Here are some suggestions for a mini-respite during your busy day.

- Take five minutes when you awaken to greet the glorious sunrise and to observe the beauty of your surroundings—clouds, fresh air, the soil beneath your feet, even the raindrops touching your face.

- Take a short "meditation" walk at coffee break time or for the first ten minutes of your lunch break. Focus on some incredibly small wonder—a tiny flower or plant growing, a bird searching for food, ripples in a puddle of water—to clear and still your mind.

- Turn off cell phones, answering machines, and TVs and sit quietly for fifteen minutes a day to encourage your mind to listen to the music inside you, the natural rhythm of your life.
- Don't just stand there, sing and dance to the radio or that CD you're playing. Free the child within!
- Each night before retiring, write down in a "joy journal" the best things that happened to you during the day and those things for which you are most grateful. Before closing your eyes at the end of the day, picture those you hold dear and embrace them with a smile and a prayer for their happiness and for the peace and well-being of the whole world.

It takes only a little time to open your soul's window and create an island of peace to nourish your beautiful self. When you do, a whole new life of healing, wonder, and joy is waiting just for you!

Please Touch

*L*ook to do some caregiving every day. Possibilities for outreach are endless for ways that we can touch with love. There are children, our families, communities, those who are ill or depressed, the homeless, orphans, and *you*! Caregiving is often discovered in unexpected places.

I was in the hospital in need of a spinal tap. The doctors tried five times to drain fluid. It was agony. Slowly, the intern reached out to hold my hand. It was the first time I remember someone reaching out to care. I cried.

Later in my life, I was being prepared for an operation. Before anesthesia, the nurse cradled my head in her arms as she told me she had the same operation, and she was fine.

My son David was critically ill with AIDS. My shift with

him at the hospital was from 2:00 a.m. until 5:00 a.m. I was with him each night and I held his hand the whole time. If I tried to relinquish my hold, he held my hand even harder.

After David died, I met a woman who asked me, "How are you doing?" Angrily, I replied, "I'm fine." The tears flowed from both of us as she told me about her son. We were two mothers who were sharing our grief together.

At another time, Nana didn't speak. The family dutifully came to visit as she sat in her chair. She didn't respond, so after a couple of sentences, they conversed with the nurses. I made a plan. I pulled up a chair directly in front of her and began relating all about the family, the company, and friends she knew. Her face lit up. We enjoyed many times together. Her mind cleared from being bored to being challenged.

Here are suggestions for helping those in need in times of trial.

- Never take away a person's right to do things for themselves.
- Tune in to nonverbal messages. Listen to emotions. Give comfort through your eyes, smiles, tears, touch.
- Talk about the illness. What are you feeling and what are they feeling?

- Ask what you can do for them.
- Bring in children to be part of the caregiving process. Tell them what is happening; share thoughts and ask them to share their feelings. Show them love, compassion, and understanding.

When you experience an ill person being agitated or angry:

- Try not to fix everything.
- Role-play. Get into the person's head to try to feel what they are going through.
- Try to understand the person even though they are not doing and saying the things you want them to do and say.
- Be a good listener.
- Be respectful and encouraging.
- Help illumine their spirit by reminding them of the beauty in nature and sharing love.
- Help them to visualize their blessings.

Recently, I went to visit LifePath, a home that cares for children with multiple health difficulties. I was deeply touched by the dignity and love with which the caregivers treated these children. The children's love was reflected back in the smiles that poured forth from their little faces.

Honor your own health in stressful times. Nana often told me that you have to take care of yourself first before you can take care of others.

- Soul-search to ask what you can do for yourself.
- Remember to laugh.
- Don't overload your "to do" list.
- Keep your life in balance. You do have a choice.
- Take walks discovering the beauty of each new day.
- Keep a personal journal of striving for inner peace and relaxation.
- Remember that it's okay to cry.

There is a wonderful children's story about a mother who had a beautiful baby boy. As she rocked him and held him close, she whispered, "I'll love you forever." She nurtured him through all stages of life. The son grew up, left home, and had a family of his own. His mother became ill, and in the final passage, the son rocked his mother in his lap and comforted her with the words, "I'll love you forever."

HUNGER FOR MEANING

eople today are searching for a deeper meaning to life. I had a lot of time to think about this while on a ten-day vacation to Maui. I left home feeling very tired and overwhelmed with too many things to do. I felt as if my goals were falling by the wayside and that I was drowning in a sea of frantic daily living. Do you ever feel like this?

We all need time to step away and re-evaluate life. For me it didn't happen the first day. It was surprising how long it took to calm down. It took quiet moments, listening to the swaying rhythm of Hawaiian music, seeing the palm trees whose branches looked like giant feathers, walking the beach, watching the waves roll to the shore, and seeing loving faces. My eyes and ears and heart beheld these wonders, and I thought about how we might bring more meaning to our lives. As I get older, time becomes more precious, and I notice priorities are changing. I feel a deep need for re-evaluation.

Our inner energy can give us the strong desire and purpose to make a positive difference in other people's lives as well as our own. Here are some ideas to help you find meaning in life.

- Breathe deeply and take time to appreciate all the beauties of nature.
- Exercise outside each day if possible. Listen to nature's music, look up at the sun and the clouds, and appreciate the awesome colors of the world around you.
- Write down your goals and put them in a place where you can see them every day.
- Take time each day to be thankful for the gift of life and all the benefits you reaped that day. Be thankful, too, for obstacles you encountered because they help you learn and grow.
- Treat yourself with kindness; you are a special person.
- Take time each day for silence so that you can hear your own inner voice of wisdom.
- Give yourself time to renew your imagination and

leave open spaces for creative thought to fill your mind. Make way for your life to be a path of light as you move forward.

🕊 There are few things as rewarding as knowing you have been instrumental in helping someone improve their life. Look for the angel in others.

🕊 Let your love shine straight from your heart and surround what you love—whether it be an adult, a child, the need for family togetherness, or our beautiful world.

A smile on your face may show that you are enjoying the moment, but the spark of life within your eyes is a message to all that you know the joy of living.

Albert Einstein said, "The intuitive mind is a sacred gift, the rational mind a loyal servant. Our society has honored the servant and forgotten the gift."

Let's honor the gift that we all have to share to bring peace and love to our troubled world. 🌹

Two Gardens

*K*ay Redfield Jamison is a professor of psychiatry at the Johns Hopkins School of Medicine in Baltimore. She writes: "It is the infectious energies of exuberance that proclaim and disperse much of what is marvelous in life."

That's how I feel—especially during spring. Imagine the most beautiful colorful garden laden with lush growing plants! It is filled with perennials, annuals, and evergreens. It is peaceful, joyful, and we have the opportunity to be our own master gardeners! It is a time of planting and anticipating the joy of bringing colorful beauty to our outside world. We have been entrusted with a treasured gift. It requires love, tenderness, understanding, and the knowledge of how to care.

At the same time there is an exciting opportunity to plant your inner garden. In our fast-paced living today, we have often become disconnected from the balance and harmony in life. Think of yourself as an orchestra leader. Each part of your body needs to play in harmony if you are to create a masterpiece.

Michael Samuels, MD, and Mary Rockwood Lane, RN, PhD, wrote *Spirit Body Healing*. They are pioneers in the field of mind-body medicine. By showing readers how to deepen the spiritual dimension in their daily lives, the authors teach them how to heal physical illness. Healing takes place when creativity is awakened in the spirit— especially through music, art, and nature.

In the book there is a wonderful spiritual meditation called "bringing in the light." It is a practice that concentrates on bringing light and love into your life. It brings incredible energy to you for healing; it surrounds you with light that comes up from the earth and down from the sky at once. When you bring in the light, you are also bringing in healing vision; you are calling your spirit to open your eyes and see.

Tending your nature's garden and your inside garden means you can be lifted up, and, when you tune into the light inside you, your flowers will grow more beautiful each day of your life! ✤

SILENCE—A GIFT

*H*ow much of your day is filled with iPods, computers, TV, cell phones, video games, radios, and traffic noise? I often think of my mother's words, "What's all this noise?"

In a study of more than 1,300 people, those who regularly used cell phones or pagers experienced an increase in psychological distress and a decrease in family satisfaction compared to those who used these devices less often, according to Noelle Chesley, a professor of sociology at the University of Wisconsin–Milwaukee.

Pete Townshend, guitarist for rock band The Who, developed severe hearing loss by using headphones and, on his Web site, warns adults and children who use personal music devices to turn down the volume or risk permanent damage.

Some studies link electromagnetic frequencies (EMF)—like those emitted by high-tech equipment—to weakened brain waves and nerve signals causing stress and fatigue.

A 2004 Harris Interactive survey of more than 1,550 people found that 46 percent of Americans say their stress level is higher now than five years ago. Eighty percent experience medium or high stress levels at work, and 60 percent experience these same stress levels at home.

Andrew Weil said, "Electromagnetic pollution may be the most significant form of pollution human activity has produced in this century, all the more dangerous because it is invisible and insensitive."

How can we counteract all these forces?

My youngest grandchild was having trouble sleeping at night, and it became a real problem. Her parents finally said she couldn't play any video games after dinner, and, miraculously, she returned to sleeping soundly through the night a short time later.

After reading that magnets may stabilize some of the forces from EMF stress, I began wearing a magnet twenty-four hours a day. My stress level is down, and my sleeping pattern is much improved.

Meditation brings peace, clears our minds, and opens our hearts, allowing creative new ideas to spring forth. Be silent. It's the "pause that refreshes."

Go for a walk, run, or bike ride. Leave your earphones behind and listen to your heart as you surround yourself with the beauty of nature, chirping birds, laughing children, and the hush of early morning.

Nurturing your spirit is the real source of healing and strength for your body. At day's end, when I sit on my deck with Puss Cat on my lap, my world is quiet. We purr together and silence brings us peace.

Part 6

FEELING THE SEASONS

A SUMMER TO CHERISH

How many times have you said, "This is one summer I will enjoy." You have great dreams of all the things you would like to do, but for some reason duties bog you down and the summer has passed by.

I suspect the "have to's" have taken priority, but when you analyze what you do every day, how much is really that important?

Stop! Break free of that "stressed out" syndrome by scrapping some of those things on your "to do" list. Are they really necessary? For example, do you really have to fix your bed every day?

When I was a Girl Scout, there was a song we sang as we sat in a circle. Each of us would take off one shoe and pass it around the circle as we sang, "We will pass the shoe, from me to you to you. Just pass the shoe, and do just what I do." We put a lot of energy into this song, but we weren't *doing* anything—just going around in a circle. Don't waste precious time passing the shoe!

Be awake to your fondest desires. Give yourself the gift of *freedom* from the monotony of mundane tasks to inspire new and fresh ideas that will fill your spirit.

Think back to wonderful times you had in childhood and relive some of those simple pleasures that bring you relaxation. Look around as if you were seeing your world for the first time. Recapture that feeling of being free with the breezes blowing through your hair. Imagine pictures in the clouds, and feel the exhilaration of seeing a beautiful sunset or sunrise. Breathe deeply and let nature give you a high!

In looking through my old diary from 1983, I found a notation I'd like to share with you.

> *Sometimes I view my life as a snail—outgrowing my shell. Other times, I feel like a butterfly, not growing another shell but bursting out to be free! Along with freeing ourselves, we can become the vehicle for helping others to realize their freedom as well. Freedom never forgets the freedom for growth for all persons.*

Write down those things you really *want* to do this summer and award yourself the time to actually do them. Eliminate the words "some day" from your vocabulary and enjoy this season of warmth and light to the fullest. Give yourself a hug—and an enormous smile. *You can* have an unbelievable summer to cherish!

COME, LITTLE LEAVES

"Come, little leaves," said the wind one day,
"Come over the meadows with me, and play;
Put on your dresses of red and gold;
Summer is gone, and the days grow cold."

—George Cooper

*I*magine a perfect autumn day! It is truly a magical time of year with trees dressed in their finest array of colors—gold, green, orange, and red. There are so many things to be thankful for. The changing seasons help us to evaluate where we have been, what we want to remember, and how we plan to grow.

As I watch the dance of the falling leaves, I think of how short their lives are—perhaps six months. The sun is playing hide-and-seek with them, peeping in and out of billowing clouds in a bright, blue sky. It's like life—sun and shadow, happiness and sadness, strength and weakness.

But right now as I walk over the farm, I throw back my head with happiness in my heart, and, as I always do every Fall, I repeat the "Come, Little Leaves" poem that I had to memorize in second grade. I have many thoughts as I watch the leaves. To me they are so much more interesting than when everything is just green. I like to think that all the spectacular colors represent the people of the world. We all have different wants and needs, opinions and cultures, but we all come from the same root of humanity: the trunk of the tree of life.

Then I ask myself, "Do the leaves know how it feels to bid farewell to the warmth of the sun? Do they realize that as they fall, they mingle with the earth to nourish the tree that has been their mother?" Their lives have a purpose, just as our lives do. Leo Buscaglia wrote a touching book for all ages about this subject and called it *The Fall of Freddie the Leaf.*

Autumn also is a time to prepare for an inward journey and give time to personal reflection. I like to think that, just as the leaves fall, our own regrets and sadness can fall away from our inner tree, which is really ourselves, and be swept away by the invigorating breeze of renewed hope. We can feel lighthearted and happy again as we move forward toward the new year to come.

Remember the dance of the beautiful falling leaves and the lessons they teach of uplifting the spirit so that you can paint a picture of their glory to hold in the center of your heart all year long.

WINTER SOLSTICE

aul Winter and Friends has a gorgeous musical album called *Celtic Solstice*. The first instrumental on the recording is "Triumph." It reminds me of a quiet spirit and a beautiful awakening of the soul.

December 20th is the longest night of the year, and the day has the least amount of sunlight. The outer darkness is an opportunity to look inward to discover how you can nourish yourself. Ask, "Who am I? What is my reason for being?" Take time to write down your thoughts.

We know that internal stress can affect our immune systems. Negative messages are detrimental to our health. How about analyzing old family patterns and hurts and challenging some outdated beliefs? This can be a time to take winter's journey to inner creativity and abundance. In a sense, this is like housecleaning. *You* can make room for bringing the sunlight inside of you to help bring healing to your body, mind, and spirit.

> *"And the ancient one waits*
> *For the young one to knock upon the door*
> *And both of them are me."*

—Danaan Parry, *The Essene Book of Days*, 1996

This is also a time of light being born again for another year. I think of a long-ago poem my mother had that suggests, "wash over me and clean my mind and heart." Rejoice in the time of promise as we face the light.

> *Reach out with understanding,*
> *positive joy,*
> *healing relationships,*
> *unconditional love,*
> *and peace!*

The more we share, the more we have. May the tools of compassion, service, and humility live in our hearts.

A few years ago, in December, my family and I went to the Winter Solstice concert by Paul Winter at the Cathedral Church of Saint John the Divine in New York City. It was so beautiful. It sent shivers up and down my spine. At the very end of the moving program in the rear of the huge cathedral, a magnificent sun rose slowly to the peak of the tall Gothic arch. Tears came to the eyes of the audience. This was the triumph of light!

And, again, Danaan Parry's words from the same book for December 30th are:

> *My heart swells with Thanksgiving*
> *For a winter of inner preparation*
> *Which will lead me to the first step*
> *In becoming a channel for peace . . .*
> *Within my own being."*

And my love to you!

Waking Up

Please place your hands over your heart.
Slowly take three deep breaths!
As you exhale, say to yourself, "I am alive!"

As the earth wakes up, I, too, am waking up to a new spring in my life! Each day is filled with opportunities, inviting us to express our own creativity. We can discover the exhilaration of each moment by opening our hearts and our senses to the changes taking place around us!

Did you notice that the days are becoming longer, and the sunshine encourages us to witness all the beauty of new growth? The birds sing their new songs as they herald this new season. There is a stirring in the soil that nourishes the bulbs and other plant life to awaken in the garden. Please smell the moisture in the earth and taste the sweetness of the air! The roots of the trees are beginning to send the sap that is their lifeblood to rise up and feed sprouting leaves. A long time ago, I read that by circling your arms around a tree, you can actually feel the sap rising. I have often experienced this with my dawn redwood tree! Hug your favorite tree to see if you can feel its life coursing, too.

Look around as if you are seeing all this amazement for the first time. As you try to live one day at a time, you will feel calmness, and your heart will be filled with peace.

Repeat this mantra to yourself each morning as you greet the daylight: "Today I will put first things first. I will honor and respect myself and stay close to what keeps me connected physically to the people surrounding me. I will open my eyes to behold all the amazing sights that I took for granted. I will reach out to touch with more understanding and forgiveness and love.

May my eyes be filled with sunshine to invigorate every part of my body, mind, and spirit. I am healthy and well and full of love!"

"We are here for a reason. I believe a bit of the reason is to throw little torches out to lead people through the dark."

—Whoopi Goldberg

"The longer I live, the more beautiful life becomes."

—Frank Lloyd Wright

CELEBRATE

At this beautiful springtime of year, everything in the garden is beginning to come alive. I wake up at dawn. I hear the roosters crow on the farm and marvel at the singing birds and the feeling of my body bursting with aliveness. Every sunrise is a start of a new day to be filled with the joy of reaching out with tenderness and being grateful for the good we can share with others.

Recently, our company decided to give me a spectacular birthday party. All the employees were invited to a luncheon celebration in our largest cafeteria. When I arrived, I was stunned to see the biggest birthday cake I had ever seen; it was made up of nine sheet cakes! All along the wall behind the cake were display boards filled with colored paper butterflies—one each from every employee. On those 8 × 8-inch butterflies that had been sent out the week before the party, each person wrote their birthday message to me. There were hundreds of good wishes, many with photos, drawings, cutout decorations, and inspirational quotes. The creativity was spectacular! I felt so loved!

I came home and put all those precious butterfly messages on a silver tray because they deserved the best. Each day I read one or two and feel lifted up. I think I have enough to last a whole year! From time to time, I share some of the messages of hope, love, and encouragement with employees via e-mail so that these special thoughts may inspire them, too.

The message of the butterfly is so encouraging. Its gentle touch is a gift; it is the vision of transformation that is possible for each of us on a personal level and within our families, the community, and the world.

Dr. Robert Snetsinger, a retired entomologist at Penn State University, has become an expert in creating butterfly gardens. He does this as a labor of love and dedicates his efforts to a daughter he lost to cancer. His story not only gives hope but also shows us how gardens can heal the gardener and the world at the same time.

One of my butterfly messages contained a quote from Nathaniel Hawthorne, "Happiness is like a butterfly which, when pursued, is always beyond our grasp, but, if you will sit down quietly, may alight upon you."

You can be like the butterfly. The joy of life can lift you up to give your spirit wings. 🦋

THE SPIRIT GARDEN

I wonder what goes on in the minds of little seeds as they push themselves toward the light. Their life begins in the womb of the earth. Are they glad to feel the warm sunlight? Do they smile inside themselves as they push out and upward to grow? Gardens lift our spirits. The beauty of plants makes us feel good. Many of us are lucky to have enough land surrounding us to plant our gardens. A garden penetrates the deepest life energies of the earth itself, and, when we're in a garden, our spirits absorb that energy. A garden at its root is a place to bring the regenerative capacity of nature close to us and create a healing strength to be part of our daily life.

Organic gardeners choose to honor nature's energy by keeping it pure. Poisoning the environment of beautiful flowers or luscious vegetables has no place in organic garden habits.

For those of us who have no space for gardening outdoors, how about planting a garden in our hearts? We could keep it pure and poison-free by planting kindness, honesty, joy, happiness, and caring for others' peace. Each day we can watch our inner gardens flourish with love and be charged with the energy to reach out and make a difference in ourselves, our families, and the world.

Another miracle garden has been planted in my daughter's life. She is forty-four years old, the mother of two daughters, and, recently, to her great surprise, she discovered that a loving seed has been planted and is growing in her womb.

In the March–May 2005 issue of *Shift* magazine there was a fascinating article by Richard Heinberg titled "Creativity Begins in the Womb." He said, "We are learning that babies come into the world with well-developed senses of touch, taste, and hearing; they move in response to pleasant or unpleasant stimuli and respond to emotions; they smile and cry even in the womb; they are already social beings, capable of interacting, imitating, and showing affection; and they are already learning about themselves and their environments." 🐿

Sanctum

by Beulah B. Malkin

I built a tiny garden
In a corner of my heart
I kept it just for lovely things
And bad all else depart
And ever was there music,
And flowers blossomed fair;
And never was it perfect
Until you entered there.

Part 7

TAKING ACTION

OUR CROSSROADS

*R*ight now, each one of us is faced with a tremendous challenge! A nation's greatest treasure is not in its power or wealth but in its people—their potential strength and basic goodness. Perhaps our biggest enemy today is complacency.

I see two alternatives in our world right now. The first is destructive behavior that reaps anger. It appears the world today is filled with anger, which breeds violence, hatred, war, and despair. These forces are not only coming from outside us but also from inside through our own fear, intolerance, anger, and discrimination. We attract what we think!

The second alternative is constructive behavior, which is filled with goodness and hope and can reach out to help other people.

The Dalai Lama said, "What has happened cannot be undone. But we as human beings have to go on with life and look to the future with a fresh mind and renewed confidence." He also said, "Peace will not come from the sky!"

Susan Skog in her book *Peace in Our Lifetime* wrote that we have to take responsibility for building a peaceful culture, beginning with our own thoughts and actions. We have to make our homes, schools, workplaces, and communities the "Camp Davids" at which we negotiate peace. We have to elect leaders who want peace as much as we do. We have to hold peace in our own lives.

"Peace is as much about getting the bombs out of our own hearts as out of the Pentagon budget," says peace educator and former *Washington Post* columnist Colman McCarthy. Anger is ravaging far too many areas of the earth. Every one of us is paying too high a price financially, physically, and emotionally for this fury.

I attended a conference where Patricia Aburdene, a renowned motivational speaker, argued that humanity has reached the turning point in economic history where there can be no prosperity without spiritual values. We need honesty to survive!

Peace is freeing our hearts to burn with love instead of hate. Whether in our personal relationships or in how we as a nation deal with other countries, when we stop harming one another and begin to honor our precious connections—even if we disagree—we will have peaceful lives.

Please get out and take a stand for the good of our nation and each other. So many people have died for the right to vote. Use your voice where it really counts!

You Can Be an Entrepreneur

My dictionary defines an entrepreneur as one who carries out any project that requires boldness and who has an adventurous spirit or energy.

Every year I attend the conference of the Leading Women Entrepreneurs of the World. New honorees are added annually, and now we are just over three hundred strong from all parts of the world. It is amazing to discover what vitality, perseverance, and integrity these women have as they pursue their dreams and become winners.

Each past honoree had a chance to speak and relate what motivated her to be a winner. Here are some of their responses.

- Believe in yourself.
- Find your own center.
- People are not holding you back—you hold yourself back.
- You are remarkable.
- Bring in your own essence to share.
- Reach out to help each other.
- Re-energize yourself with the spirit.
- Pretend you have done it before.
- Try new things.
- We are partners.
- Crisis reveals character.
- When we experience failure, begin again more intelligently.
- From every challenge we can grow stronger.
- Learn to share.
- Always have impeccable manners and show respect and courtesy towards others.
- "You can count on me!"
- Lift each other up.

In just about every response, the speaker expressed a strong desire to give back to the community. Their energy and experience gave them the drive to make the world a better place.

Every year, the attendees are busy taking photos of the panoramic beauty of that year's locale (Bermuda and Bangkok, to name a couple), but it's like focusing on the world through a telescope. We needed to broaden our view, to turn our minds to experience what we feel, and then turn our hearts to discover love and understanding.

This is what we all need to do: Be entrepreneurs and encourage others—our spouses, children, and friends—to live with that kind of adventurous spirit. In this way, we can spread kindness, understanding, love, beauty, and joy to our families, communities, and the world.

Someone once asked Helen Keller what could be worse than being blind. Her response was, "Having sight but no vision."

We are all ordinary people with extraordinary opportunities. Dream big! Be bold! Go for it! Your energy and spirit will make a difference. You can do it! 🌾

PERSONAL MAGNETISM

*A*re you ready for a change? Every now and then it is time for our hearts and souls to search out new direction. It is a call from nature to do some spiritual cleaning. Do you feel this challenge?

These past few months I have been doing a lot of reading about a particular kind of renewable energy, and guess what? It's all free! There is growing evidence that an electromagnetic field surrounds and connects all of us.

When you went to school, do you remember the experiments that you did with magnets in science class? You learned what types of things were attracted to or repelled by the magnet. I never imagined then that it could affect our bodies, too. They didn't teach us that next step.

The electromagnetic field surrounding our body is called an aura. We can be drained or invigorated, and here's how!

Depression, fear, anger, frustration, envy, sadness, grief, and worry as well as an "I can't do it" attitude dim our auras and drain our energy. Often shallow breathing takes place when we are in this negative state, and we feel run down and sometimes weak. Living with these traits on a continued basis can make our bodies vulnerable to illness.

On the other hand, happiness, hope, joy, dreams, laughter, reaching out to others, physical exercise, goal setting, enthusiasm, and looking forward to the future make our auras strong and vibrant, and we seem radiant with good health and confidence.

You decide! Feel the exhilaration of deep breathing and inner positive power that can awaken your mind, heart, and spirit to all the good that surrounds you. The question facing you is what do you want to attract? Make your list and concentrate on drawing those positive things into your life.

Make your aura shine! We have free will. We can program our journey as we move forward. May your journey be one filled with the magnetism of positive power and love!

SAVE OUR PLANET

What a tremendous sacred gift we have been given to live in this beautiful world! Do we hold it dear to our hearts, or do we take it for granted?

Aristotle said, "In all things of nature there is something marvelous."

What has happened in our world? I am dismayed when I read in the newspapers that, for many, ethics have been put aside in favor of greed and financial gain.

The Very Reverend Dean James Morton, retired head of the Cathedral Church of Saint John the Divine in New York, has said that our earth was formed as a sacred space, a cloak that protects us with a life-giving atmosphere, a cloak that protects a vast myriad of plants and animals that depend on each other for survival. He believes we have abused its sacredness and are ruining our soil and water with chemicals, garbage, and pollutants. Forests have been razed around the world and cities have been built too close to the floodplains. If we don't mend our environmental cloak around the world, Dean Morton asks, how will we live? How will we survive? What do we hold dear? How can we change our consciousness to become better stewards for the future? Can we envision our earth without boundaries that divide us? How can we love our neighbors who have different cultures from ours? He says each one of us needs to take up our needle to mend those deepened holes!

Experience teaches us that if we try to dominate our environment, we will never win. We need positive changes in human attitudes, and each of us needs to speak out. We have to turn from a battle against nature to appreciation for and partnership with nature. We need to let our lawmakers know how we feel.

Some magazines tell personal stories about people who are changing the world. *You* can make a difference, too, by raising your voice against the practices that cause environmental damage, needless wars, and large-scale suffering throughout the world.

Recently I looked out the window to see our magnificent red beech tree. I saw the trunk as the body with a sad face. The branches were like arms—some weak, some strong—reaching out in all directions. It reminded me of the plight of our earth. My heart breaks when I see suffering here and abroad. Peace is cheaper than war.

Never forget that in preserving the environment and fostering peace and love in the world we protect our most precious resource—our children, grandchildren, and all generations to come. As we make efforts to heal the earth, let's remember also to reach out to heal each other, one by one, forming a strong chain for peace.

Take a stand! Speak out with love and understanding to your families, communities, and the world. Get involved!

OUR WORLDWIDE FAMILY

'd like to welcome you with great excitement to our expanding Rodale family and share with you an amazing experience. Recently I attended Rodale's International Sales Conference in Mexico. Our magazines already enjoy a robust presence worldwide with fifty-five editions in forty-eight countries. Even though we come together from different continents, we are not so far away from each other: We touch; we care; we love!

I have attended all of these conferences, and each year I see wide-eyed, energetic people who are focused and radiating a positive force that emerges from their spirit. Each member of the group respects the others as we work together to promote good health, unity, and togetherness.

These sessions could be a wonderful example to governments all over the world. Here is a part of my message to those who attended the conference:

As we move forward, we continually strive for fresh ideas so that our readers and we ourselves will be inspired for a happy, healthy life.

I was so excited about all our partners and their new ideas. It is the soul of the editors and staff to take the American magazines and perfect them for their own market.

Men's Health *South Africa said, "It's your life. Make it good!"*

Reach out and touch to make a difference with love. We are like fingers stretching out with our messages of living a special, whole life.

When you're faced with a challenge, climb out of the valley to conquer the mountaintop.

Breathe in with exhilaration the far-reaching vistas of expanding dreams.

Believe that your dreams have already happened. Say "YES" in your heart that you have already received the reality of your desires.

Look at each person as a treasured light to illuminate the world.

Be thankful for your gift to reach out to make a difference.

Balance your mind, body, and spirit. Be the instrument to play beautiful music that touches the heartstrings of others.

Each morning, I was awestruck by the majestic cruise ships sailing into harbor. I watched them with tear-filled eyes and thought of each of our member countries as a ship of hope. May we all be vehicles carrying health, healing, and peace to our entire expanding world. Wherever you journey, dear reader, carry your mission onward.

My heart reaches out to each one of you, and I pray for your safety and well-being. Bless you all!

The Eye of Intuition

*D*o you realize that the one-dollar bill has a third eye? It is located in a triangle surrounded by the rays of a sunburst. It is the eye of intuition that connects the triangle of our eye to see, our ears to hear, and our heart to feel to a deeper level. We can become our own physician, healing the mind, body, and spirit.

We should use our third eye as a guide for our intuitive thoughts. Most often our intuition will lead us to the deeper understanding of who we are and how we can let our light shine.

Our third ear is there for us to realize the importance of listening closely to what people say and to practice silence in order that new inspiration can challenge us to be a vehicle to spread peace and understanding to each other and the world.

Jean Shinoda Bolen, MD, psychiatrist, said in her article "Choosing the Path with the Heart," "What talents did we come with? What do we find fascinating? What gives us joy? What do we know matters deeply to us? If we are spiritual beings on a human path, the answers to the questions that shape the journey do not come from outside of us, for the wisdom that knows is within us. . . . It is the journey, not the destination that matters."

This morning as I finished my daily exercises and affirmations, I raised my hands over my head and then slowly brought them down in front of me in a prayerful position over my heart. As I did so, I realized I was looking to my third eye to enlighten my eyes, ears, and heart to a deeper meaning of life and outreach to others.

The call of listening to our intuition can open up our minds to look beyond ourselves, and the community, families, and the world in which we live. With compassion we have seen the tragedy of the South Asian earthquake and tsunami, the devastation of war-torn countries, and the grief of losing those we love. We need to know in our hearts how dependent we are on each other and not be polluters of our intuition.

The Dalai Lama said in his *Words of Wisdom*, "We can share the earth and take care of it together, rather than trying to possess it, destroying the beauty of life in the process."

Let's be citizens of the world!

HEALING THE WORLD

hroughout time, people and nations have tried to solve problems by force. Did these people know the tender touch of love? Were they treated with love? What about their families? I often wonder what they were like. Were they poor? Were they wealthy? Did they have troubled child-hoods? Did anyone ever ask these questions, or were the troublemakers just assumed to be bad and then forgotten?

When I married, my father-in-law J. I. Rodale told me, "I am so happy that you have joined our family—it is now a melting pot with Jewish, Catholic, and Protestant heritage." He realized that one of the greatest gifts is understanding the value of peace and compassion. From him, I learned unity and harmony of the mind, body, and spirit. All life is sacred, and, when we are silent and become part of that peace, nature can be the orchestra leader to help us heal. I discovered the inner being of my soul. My body has become vibrant, and I am filled with energy and light.

We need to work together to nurture the soul of each individual and spread the message of peace, understanding, and love. The world cannot exist without these. We should cherish each other and help regenerate the world with care and kindness instead of war and destruction. Albert Pine said it beautifully: "What we do for ourselves dies with us. What we do for others and the world remains and is immortal."

Mokichi Okada was a poet, artist, mystic, visionary, businessman, husband, father, and spiritual teacher. He envisioned creating a world of peace, health, and prosperity for us all—a paradise on Earth: 🍃

Born
As human beings,
It is our duty
To strive our utmost
For peace in the world
And the happiness of others.
Those
Who love humanity
And help people in need,

Are always loved
And protected by God
Wherever they may go.
A person
Who strives constantly
To help others
And better the world,
Is like a diamond
Buried in the sand.

PRECIOUS GARDEN
OF HOPE

*G*ardening has always played an important part in my life. A few years ago, I was very stressed. A young farmer who worked for us gave me invaluable advice. He said, "Ardie, go to your garden and dig, and you'll see your problems will find some answers." At first, I dug ferociously, and gradually the tension lessened. I started to find peace, and answers started to surface. As fresh air and oxygen invigorated every part of my body, I began to heal.

In 1984 in California, I met an amazing woman, Cathrine Sneed. She had an idea and went to the sheriff of San Francisco to propose a jailhouse community garden now called The Garden Project. More than twenty years later, there has been a 95 percent reduction in their repeat offender cycle as The Garden Project helps inmates learn important social skills by working with different people, being responsible employees, and moving on to achieve more productive lives. The food they grow in their gardens is distributed to needy people, and often it is the first time in the inmates' lives that they have done something good for others and contributed to society. The Garden Project is now a model for preventing crime and building self-esteem. It has been so successful that many participants have moved on to start their own businesses. They have discovered that gardening can nourish their bodies as well as their souls. Cathrine has said, "We are giving the inmates a sense of responsibility. We just don't grow plants, we grow people. Gardening has given them hope."

Imagine what you can do! Be an entrepreneur in your community and help to decrease the growing number of at-risk youths. Volunteer at your local community garden or food bank and take the opportunity to intervene and reclaim young people from lives of poverty and despair. Let's help heal our society by giving those young people hope and a sense of family, peer, and community support.

You'll see something amazing happen—a shift in attitude and behavior from being victims to becoming proactive, responsible citizens. You will give them the ability to dream, and enjoy a sense of accomplishment. Plant gardens *and* love! 🌸

To contribute to The Garden Project, visit their Web site at www.gardenproject.org or write to them at The Garden Project, PO Box 24292, San Francisco, CA 94124.

Part 8
DREAMING

SITTING IN A SUNBEAM

When I was a child, I often welcomed the sunbeam as it flooded through our living room window. I would see myself sitting in that sunbeam trying to catch the shining particles of dust in my hands. This was dreamtime for me. I would feel the inner powerhouse of imagination, warmth, love, and peace. Perhaps this dreamtime was spurred on by a song we used to sing, "Jesus Wants Me for a Sunbeam." I don't remember the other words, but the message of sharing light in our lives really stuck.

One of my daily calendar pages held the message, "To hope and dream is not to ignore the practical. It is to dream in colors and rainbows."

Today, I spend my dreamtime walking and sitting in quiet meditation in my sunroom as I plan ways that I can make these dreams a reality. Dreams are like planting seeds and patiently waiting for them to grow as we nurture and refine their fruition.

I think a lot about my husband, Bob, and the legacy he left behind. He, too, did a lot of his dreaming while walking the fields. His ideas and dreams also came from conversations with people. I believe he knew the value of that verse from the Bible, "Ask and you shall receive."

There came a time in Bob's life where he felt constricted by business procedures, so he took time to explore other cultures and sought out visionary friends. Often his path led him through winding roads instead of a highway as he gleaned ideas and dreams from what he discovered along the way. He was a painter, a photographer, and, as the years went by, he shared his artistry in new ways. He preached and dreamed of a whole new, regenerated land where we could take the best from the past to create a New World Symphony to make it a safer, more caring place—a land where everyone would unite to bring better health to all people. He left me with the urgency to carry on and enlarge the dream.

There is a special quote by Lewis Carroll in *Through the Looking-Glass*: "He was part of my dream, but then I was part of his dream, too."

When you dream, you have the opportunity to nurture your whole self—your heart, your soul, and your body. You have the opportunity to enrich other people's lives. Touch, feel, become a part of what you are creating.

I guess I will always be a child at heart when I remember simple pleasures like sitting in the sunbeam. I have been buying solar rainbow makers to give to children as gifts. They are attached to a window where sun is shining through by a suction cup. Rainbows spin all around the room, and with excitement people of all ages cry, "Wow!"

Langston Hughes said, "Never lose hope in your dreams. For without dreams, life is a broken-winged bird that cannot fly."

Give yourself the joy and time to dream!

THE ELEGANT SPIRIT

Whenever I asked "How are you today?," my neighbor's response was always the same, "Only medium."

Do you hear other people who continually have a "Woe is me" attitude? Do they feel old?

My eight-year-old granddaughter and I had a discussion of what it means to be old, and I realized we were two worlds apart. To her, it meant someone who looks worn out. I told her two things. First, some people are old at twenty. Second, oldness happens when a person loses sight of dreams, regardless of the number of years they have lived.

We continue to need time to re-evaluate our lives. What

happens in Mother Earth is a perfect example for what can happen in our bodies. In the spring, bulbs and plants begin to wake up after their winter's nap. There are times in our lives when we, too, need to wake up our earth bodies with renewed optimistic nourishment.

Just as we feed our bodies when we are hungry, we need to also feed our souls. More people today have a hunger to bring more meaning into their lives. In order to do this, we need to realize that every day we have the choice to change our outlook.

Our health depends on finding new ways of addressing problems that have become a block to health and, to a large extent, to how we approach life.

In one of his books, Deepak Chopra teaches that the only reason we are not perfectly healthy is because we are always taking new bricks and putting them in old slots. Why do we do that? He says that if you look closely at your own life, you realize that you are sending signals to your body that repeat the same old beliefs, the same old fears and wishes, the same old habits of yesterday. That is why we are stuck in the same old body. But, we can change that!

Some time ago, I heard Dr. Elie Wiesel speak. He is a Nobel Peace Laureate and survivor of the Holocaust. He has a prescription for bringing about positive change. He says that we need to bring back the poetry in life, the poetry in human relations, the poetry in music, the poetry in art.

Caroline Myss, PhD, and C. Norman Shealy, MD, wrote a book, *The Creation of Health*. At the end of the book, Shealy uses a wonderful phrase—"The Elegant Spirit." I fully believe that if we can have a balance with the mind, body, and spirit, the result will be a unity of health and a beautiful appreciation for life.

Think of the wonderful opportunities we have to bring excitement and joy to life for ourselves and others. Please pick a bouquet of beautiful thoughts as you go to sleep each night. Dream about all your new ways of reaching out. Go to sleep with a smile, and you'll always be young in heart!

LIFELINE OF LOVE

The first snow squall came from the sky in a torrent, filling me with childlike excitement. I could barely see the cars on the highway near my house. Beautiful music played on the compact disc, and in my sunroom there was a warm fire glowing on the hearth. The snow falling on the sky-lights made me feel as if stars were descending rapidly from the heavens. I wanted to touch it all!

Hurrying outside, I lifted my face upward to capture the cool snowflakes on my tongue. My mind was filled with the words of Louis Armstrong singing, "I think to myself, what a wonderful world."

The night was brand new. Everything was washed clean.

Amazement filled the air as I felt the stirring of new life within.

I imagined that life was calling us to new dreams, to think new ideas, to discover new ways to care for family and friends. We need to find better ways to keep our bodies healthy and to care for our world. We need to be ambassadors of peace and healing in our troubled world. Now is the time to challenge our lives as we are filled with new energy and appreciation for all our gifts. We need to nurture these gifts like new seeds of thoughts already germinating in our minds.

There will always be other snowstorms. Enjoy each of them as contemplation time to expand all your new ideas. Inner creativity needs to grow so large that it is ready to be born in the sun. Look up and out and savor each new moment as you capture it like a snowflake—refreshing, enriching, and loving. They become nuggets of growth in our hearts.

Life is constantly changing, but some things should never change, like the feelings we have for family and friends. The bond of love is a lifeline that is always there reaching out to people who are special in our lives. Sometimes the line is held loosely, but the thoughts are there and, when the need arises, the love line tightens, and we respond to the grace that binds us together in friendship and caring. I send you my love!

May our dreams be filled to the brim with new, wonderful surprises, and may we dance in the light of oneness with new joy. Let us join hands to work for peace in our beautiful but troubled world.

> *"Let us sing a new song,*
> *not with our lips,*
> *but with our lives."*
>
> —St. Augustine

WHY ARE YOU HERE?

$\mathcal{M}$any of us go through our lives each day doing only the tasks before us without giving much thought to making longer-term goals. We are so busy rushing. Do you take time to stop and ask yourself, "Why am I here?"

I'm sure answers would vary greatly. "I have a job to do," or "I must support my family," or "I don't know why I'm here. I'm so bored! Life is the same old thing day in and day out."

How wonderful if people could answer by saying, "I have a dream and a vision. I want to make a difference in my own life. I want to feel the satisfaction of knowing that I am my best self. I want to help other people. I want to continue to learn and grow." You can be filled with wonder even on an ordinary day.

One man worked very hard seventy hours a week. When asked what was most important in his life, he answered, "Without a doubt, it's my wife and two daughters." Would his priorities match?

When I'm losing track of my dream, it's vital to *stop*, breathe deeply, and try to simplify my life, weeding out nonessentials early before their roots penetrate too deeply. To do this, I need to take time to listen with my mind *and* my heart. When we relax and focus, harmonious waves are created in life and amazing things happen.

Tony Mowbray from Australia sailed around the world alone. He spoke at one of our company's international meetings and said that by living on the edge in the vast ocean, he had lots of time to think. His experience required tremendous flexibility when facing storms, and he had to keep his focus in order to survive. He shared five important steps to accomplish any mission: Dream, Think, Talk, Commit, and Act.

He had lots of time for soul-searching, but he accomplished his dream and became a guide for his children through life even though he was away from them for nine months. They had to learn self-sufficiency in his absence. Before he left, he told his family about the stars. "You can see your star wherever you are, and the stars of those you love." May we learn from Tony.

Take time at the end of the day to review your progress toward your goals and be thankful for the good that happened during your waking hours.

Every day can be filled with meaning if you set your mind to it. When you awake in the morning, start your day by saying, "Good morning, Self! I greet you with joy in my heart, and I reach out to touch those people I encounter today with appreciation and love!" Then, you'll know *why you are here*!

DARE TO DREAM

*I*n her book, *The Invitation*, Oriah Mountain Dreamer wrote, "It doesn't interest me what you do for a living. I want to know what you ache for and if you dare to dream of your heart's longing."

Most of us spend one-third of our lives in bed! Much of that time is spent dreaming. Our dreams offer a tremendous opportunity to create a huge storehouse of ideas that could influence our lives with creativity instead of mediocrity.

My husband always kept a pen and paper by the bed to write down immediately any thoughts or dreams that came to him, fearing that, if he waited until morning, he might lose them forever. I do the same thing now!

We can also dream while we're awake. Children often

have very vivid dreams of who they want to become, but sometimes parents squelch their dreamtime. I remember my aunt doing just that to her young son. One morning he sat daydreaming by the side of his bed. When she asked what he was doing, he replied, "Dreaming about when Jane and I get married."

My aunt replied, "Come now! Do something constructive." I heard that story as a child and never forgot it.

Many times in my life, dreams have been an urgent message to contact someone who appeared in the dream. I was always sorry if I didn't contact them within a week. Sometimes, dreams are a call for immediate action.

It's been said that Einstein had a breakthrough in his theory of relativity in a dream. J. K. Rowling was staring out a train window, daydreaming, when the idea, plot, and characters for the Harry Potter books popped into her head.

Recently I visited my granddaughter's school. One wall was filled with the students' "Dare to Dream" quotes. Here are some samples:

> *"Soar with the birds above the earth and hear their wings in the wind."*

"In my dream I have the courage to attempt any new sport I wish to do. I make a promise to myself that this dream will begin this winter with skiing."

"In my dream, I am a strong and graceful dancer."

"I would love to climb Mt. Rushmore, and then hang from George Washington's nose!"

Make yourself a dream board, adding pictures, inspirational thoughts, and fun items to stimulate your creative dreaming every day. Gandhi said, "Do not curse the darkness. Instead, light a candle!"

Let your dreams light the way on your life's journey.

THE GIFT
FOR EVERY SEASON

*S*everal years ago, I received a December gift that has become part of my life and spirit every day. Gill, my grand-daughter, brought me an artificial pine tree adorned with twinkling white lights. My daughter Heather brought me the "icing"—beautiful glass Moravian stars to hang on this tree of life to represent each one of my grandchildren. I pray in my heart each day for love, health, and safety to surround them. This tree is not just for one season—it is for all seasons and will always remain visible as a part of me.

I placed the tree in the sunroom, my favorite place in the house. The room is circled on three sides with large windows that look out over our peaceful farm. It is here that I see the changing seasons and the beautiful working tree arboretum, the snow, sun, sunsets, rain, clouds, and stars.

The pine tree that I see in daylight in the sunroom changes as night descends upon the room. It is magnified from one tree into three as it is reflected in each one of the three large windows. The sparkling lights and the Moravian stars have expanded to an awesome sight!

In the corner of the room is a small green fireplace upon which stands a tall candleholder in the shape of a pine branch. It holds one lone candle. I think of myself as that candle and often ask, "Why am I here?" What does the expanded panorama of this room mean?

My mind travels back to a beloved ceremony at the camp I attended as a camper and then as a counselor. On the last night, each person received one candle mounted on a section of birchwood. After a long, silent procession to the river, each camper lit their candle and made a wish as the birchwood boat and candle were set afloat on the water. It was a humbling sight for us to watch our individual beacons of inspiration join the others as they were set afloat in the stream of life. My candle made a difference as it joined the others to create a brighter light enhancing the power of all.

My decorated pine tree and the lone candle have taken on a new significance as I see the lesson of the night. The Moravian stars are not only for my grandchildren but also for children everywhere. Each of us is a lone candle united with others to create a blazing light like the candles in the river and bring about deeper understanding and unconditional love as we spread hope for a healthier world filled with unity.

May we hold close in our arms people throughout the world who are starving, homeless, ill, lonely, or sad. Our hearts are bigger than we realize. May we each discover and share the gift of greater love in the coming years.

Photographs